To Alice,

Pamela Miner

# The Origin of Mattole

## Through the Eyes
## of a Salmon

# George "Buck" Miner

# The Origin of Mattole
## Through the Eyes of a Salmon

Copyright © 1996 by George "Buck" Miner

All rights reserved. No part of this book may be used, reproduced, or transmitted in any manner whatsoever without written permission, except in the case of brief quotations embodied in articles or reviews.

Published by
George "Buck" Miner
36328 Mattole Road
Petrolia, CA 95558

Edited by Randy Stemler

Cover Designed and Illustrated by Laura Walker

ISBN 0-9653673-0-4

# TABLE OF CONTENTS

INTRODUCTION 1

Chapter 1:
AN IDEA FOR A BOOK 3

Chapter 2:
THROUGH THE EYES OF A SALMON 5

Chapter 3:
SALMON FISH FACTS 7

Chapter 4:
POINTS OF INTEREST 9

Chapter 5:
MATTOLE GETS ITS NAME 14

Chapter 6:
FROM THE OCEAN TO
THE LOWER NORTHFORK 15
Collins Gulch; Bear Creek; Stansberry Creek; Prosper Ridge; Moore Hill; Rackliff Hole; Jim Goff Gulch; Uncle Tommy; Mill Creek; Tom Scott Creek; Titus Creek; Jeffry Gulch; Lower Northfork; Yellow Rose; Creamery Hill; Grizzly Creek; Joel Flat Creek; Hornback; Taylor Peak; Shumaker Ridge; Burnt Ranch; Walker Mountain; Fruit Ranch

Chapter 7:
PETROLIA 42
*The Town; Crane Hill*

## Chapter 8:
## LINDLEY BRIDGE TO LINDLEY BRIDGE 51

*George Lindley Bridge; The Hideaway; East Mill Creek; Apple Tree Ridge; Cady Ridge; Clear Creek; Hadley Creek; Roberts' Hole; Conklin Creek; McGinnis Creek; Wire Fence, Homestead, and Cow Pasture Openings; Goose Bend Hole; Rainbow Ridge; Buckeye Mountain; Burgess Ridge; Van Schoiack; The Peg Leg; Grooms Ridge/Everts Ridge; Sherman's Prairie; Shenanigan Ridge; The Dutchman; Jim Creek; Indian Creek*

## Chapter 9:
## NEW JERUSALEM 69

*Elwyn Lindley Bridge; Mill Creek (Another One)/Dannyville/Wild Turkey Creek; Gardner Creek/Green Fir Mill Creek/Drinking Water Creek; Cooskie Mountain; Log Cabin Hole; Annie's Cabin; Graveyard Hill; Mattole Grange Hall; New Jerusalem; Fall Creek; A. W. Way County Park*

## Chapter 10:
## SQUAW CREEK TO BULL CREEK 84

*Squaw Creek; The Concrete Arch; The Mill Pond; Mary's Flat; Hadley Hole; Bill Dudley Flat; Tom Reed Flat; Thornton Gulch and Mail Ridge; Hazel Nut Opening; The Rock House; Roscoe Ford; Pritchett Creek; Granny Creek; Damon, Harris, and Moody Ridges; Moorehead Ridge; Telegraph Ridge; Cook Gulch; Saunders Creek; Singley Creek; Hadley Creek; Coon Ridge; Holman Creek; Kendall Gulch; Dirty Creek; Spring Creek; Woods Creek; Bunnel Prairie Creek; Hunter Bluff; Divorce Flat; Parkhurst Ridge; Upper Northfork; Rainbow Ridge; Green Ridge*

## Chapter 11:
## BULL CREEK TO HONEYDEW 110

*Bull Creek Mountain; Panther Gap; Cathey's Peak and Windy Nip; Gregg Peak; Powder Flat and Nigger Heaven*

TABLE OF CONTENTS

## Chapter 12:
## HONEYDEW TO ETTERSBURG 115
*Honeydew; Honeydew Creek; Wilder Ridge; Fox Spring; Ab Creek; Big Gulch; Pringle Ridge; Dry Creek; Middle Creek; Westlund Creek; Gilham Creek; Duncan Creek/Duncan Flat/Duncan Preemption; Fourmile Creek; Phronie's Flat; Buckeye Ridge; Rail Pile Ridge; Sholes Creek; Harrow Creek; Grindstone Creek; Sterrit Hole; Doodyville; Mattole Canyon Creek; Clark's Butte; Blue Slide Creek; Greek Turn; Bear Creek*

## Chapter 13:
## ETTERSBURG TO WHITETHORN 137
*Ettersburg; Wolf Creek; Little Finley Creek and Big Finley Creek; Eubanks Creek; Nooning Creek; Sinkyone Creek; Bridge Creek; King Range; Painter Creek and McKee Creek; Vanarkin Creek; Anderson Creek; Upper Mill Creek; Harris Creek*

## Chapter 14:
## WHITETHORN TO THE HEADWATERS 154
*Whitethorn; Gibson Creek and Gibson Ridge; Stanley Creek; Baker Creek; Thompson Creek; Yew Creek; Helen Barnum Creek; Lost River Creek; Gopherville; Upper Dry Creek; Dream Stream; Arcanum Creek; Bear Paw Creek; Phillip's Creek; McNasty Creek and Ancestor Creek; Four Corners*

## Epilogue 170

## Index 173

## About the Author 180

## Mattole Watershed Map 182

# INTRODUCTION

Thank you for purchasing my first book. As you delve into these pages, don't expect to find the usual dull and boring accounts which most history books contain.

As a lad I dozed during most history lessons. I decided that if I were ever to write about history, I would attempt to enliven the past with humorous anecdotal tales that could be enjoyed, page by page, while encountering historical facts.

My ancestors came west in 1868, bringing the first covered wagons into the Mattole Valley. I have lived in the middle Mattole for more than seventy years, and still believe there is no finer place on this planet to hang your hat.

My acknowledgments are simple. If I were to follow the format of the average manuscript, I would list each person who contributed to this work. Fearing that I may leave someone out, I left you all out! Seriously though, I do appreciate each and every one of the several hundred contributors who welcomed me into their homes or talked with me on the phone or by letter. So many of these helpful people, believing that I was making a social call, soon found that I was rooting through the dusty back shelves of their memories.

    I approached Martha Roscoe (Mattole's premiere historian) with the idea for this book in the seventies, and she was delighted. She contributed much to these pages. My sincere wish is that in a century or two, when new entrants come to dwell here in the Mattole watershed, and wonder about the origin of particular names for landmarks, they can pull this book from some dusty shelf and have that curiosity satisfied.

    If you find I have overlooked your pet name for some ridge, creek, or gully, I have a forgivable reason for the omission. I probably never had the opportunity to visit with you. I have dealt mainly with the standard maps of the area, but I have also included memorabilia never documented on any maps. You can refer to your map provided in this book for general orientation and locations of most of the creeks and ridges mentioned.

    I've striven to make this an affordable manuscript, and my sincere hope is that I have provided something worthwhile for posterity. Now it's time to move along to Chapter One.

# 1

# AN IDEA FOR A BOOK

One bright sunshiny morning, while riding along with Joe Erwin over Bull Creek Mountain, I pondered a question. Finally I asked him. "Joe. You used to live up near Panther Gap. Do you know how it got its name?" He thought for awhile and then said, "I guess the same way Honeydew or Bull Creek got theirs."

For the next few minutes I sat in a quandary over the conundrum. I had lived in the Mattole Valley for over fifty years and didn't know how even one landmark had received its name. I wondered if there were folks still alive who might hold the answers. I asked Joe, my good friend who had done a bit of writing, how one goes about writing a book. "That's easy," came his reply. "You just start at the beginning and write until finished." Ironic as it seems, I took his whimsical advice and did just that.

Actually, before we completed our journey that day, we were both convinced that this book should be written. Soon the two of us were knocking on many old-timers' doors, hoping to rescue a few gems of old history for our upcoming manuscript. Unfortunately for me, Joe's work took him to the East Coast, and I have stumbled along since then, for nearly twenty years gathering historical remnants for landmark after landmark. So sit back and relax, your zany author is ready to introduce a "tail"!

# 2

# THROUGH THE EYES OF A SALMON

It was a tough decision to decide just exactly where to start this manuscript. There are three vehicle routes into the Mattole Valley. Should I choose one of these as a framework for exploring the multitude of landmarks that will eventually be presented as the book unfolds? Should I begin at the headwaters of the Mattole River, and drift seaward toward the Pacific, or would it be best to begin at the ocean and work my way to the headwaters? One day the answer came to me out of the blue — the blue Pacific Ocean.

    I was at the mouth of the Mattole River with a friend. We parked at the end of Lighthouse Road and hiked north a few hundred yards to the spot where the water of the Mattole ran through a small channel in the sand dunes and merged with the mighty Pacific. We stood back from the edge of the channel as the soft sand kept caving off and falling into the swift-moving current.

There was a splash on our left from the tail of one particular salmon. In an extra effort, she started up the Mattole on her way to spawn. As I witnessed this, lady luck smiled on me. I had been gathering history for this book for many moons without knowing how to present it, but upon seeing this salmon spawner, I was inspired, and instantly knew where to begin.

Most fishermen call a female fish a hen. The salmon we had just witnessed was a female, bearing eggs, and I dubbed her Henrietta. She would soon be in the headwaters of the Mattole. From here on, our fish friend helps us explore the history of Mattole as she splashes upstream along the entire length of the river toward its source.

# 3

# SALMON FISH FACTS

Our fish friend, Henrietta, is a member of the *Salmonidae* family. Hen, as I call her for short, has other aliases, such as spring salmon, king, Chinook, quinnat, tye, and *Oncorhynchus*, the last being the genus name meaning hook snout. I have also witnessed fishermen giving the salmon many other descriptive names, especially when a hooked fish breaks the line by diving under an object like a submerged tree trunk.

Salmon runs in the Mattole have dwindled to the point that now, in 1996, they nearly approach the status of being listed as endangered. Personally, I have not had a nibble, either on a line, or on my fork, for years.

Before Henrietta's appearance at the mouth of the Mattole, she spent five years in the ocean. Salmon spend anywhere from two to seven years in the big pond. When Hen's mother ventured up the Mattole and spawned, one of her eggs became our Henrietta. If her mother was a large fish, Hen could have from two thousand to fourteen thousand brothers and sisters. Humans have problems dealing with less than a dozen brothers and sisters. I feel fortunate not to be a fish.

In egg form, Henrietta spent fifty days or so growing in the gravel where her mother buried her. She eventually emerged from the gravel and grew into a healthy fingerling. Shortly thereafter, she migrated down to the ocean, where she roamed the foam as far north as Alaska. Now, upon her return to the mouth of the Mattole, weighing nearly fifty pounds, she is ready to start the cycle all over. If she had put on an additional thirty-five pounds, she would have rivaled one of the largest salmon on record, weighing in at more than thirty-eight kilograms (nearly 84 pounds).

In the 1860's, commercial fishing began for salmon. Between lures, nets, and aquatic predators, we're fortunate to have Henrietta to lead us through these chapters.

# 4

# POINTS OF INTEREST

Before we begin Henrietta's journey upstream, let's discuss a bit of history outside the watershed of the Mattole. If in 1543, Hen's ancestors swam around Cape Mendocino, as she just did, they could have encountered a sailing ship along this stretch of coast. These sailors were sent to this section of the Pacific to document whatever they could learn. After a time, they returned home with little to report. History books tell us they described the area that we refer to as our Lost Coast as "a desolate piece of geography." Recently, 450 years later, I spoke with a chap on a sailing ship just south of Sugar Loaf Rock. In our chat on shortwave radio he described what he was seeing landward as "a desolate piece of geography." However, history tells us that this venture north by said explorers did provide us with the name for this

*Sugar Loaf Rock at Cape Mendocino juts into the Pacific Ocean as the westernmost point of land in the lower forty-eight states.*

extreme western point of land—Cape Mendocino, named after the Spanish viceroy, Mendoza.

Between Cape Mendocino and the mouth of the Mattole River, there is a geologic formation known as Steamboat Rock. It does not take much imagination to visualize a ship.

Back in the 1940's, when Japan and the United States were lobbing old melted-down auto bodies at each other, much of our Pacific beach was patrolled by servicemen just in case of a sneak attack. Personally, I cannot conjure up any minute reason why an enemy would want to land on the Lost Coast. Being on foot, our attacker would eat all the groceries he could carry ashore before he could locate a new supply. But, the War Department said patrol, and patrol they did.

One night when it was extremely foggy, two new recruits were peering into the misty gloom and they made an astounding discovery. You guessed it! They

*With a foggy evening backdrop, the silhouette of Steamboat Rock looks just like a battleship.*

saw a destroyer right offshore. They ran right back to headquarters and called in the find. Ol' Steamboat Rock was nearly blown apart as a result. Fortunately, some person with rank discovered the error in identification, and the old rock remained.

During the summer, Steamboat Rock is treated to an off-white paint job. This work of art is donated quite freely by several hundred visiting sea gulls which perch on the old ship. I have been passing it many times a year for over half a century, and it surely must have its anchor well secured on the bottom because it has never moved one iota in all this time. However, on the morning of April 25, 1992, the old ship-like rock got a severe kick from down under. When the shaking ceased, the coastline in the vicinity had risen three or four feet skyward.

Three tectonic plates come together near this point and form the Triple Junction. One dives down under the other, and the two slide past the third to cause mass destruction for homes, roads, and general topography miles around. A few more shocks such as this, and old Steamboat Rock will be dry-docked, and those people interested in observing the landmark can do so without getting their feet wet. But to be honest, I hope I am in Denver or Toledo when that occurs.

Continuing south for a few minutes, we arrive at a group of rocks known as Mussel Ranch. The title is derived from the enormous population of shellfish clinging to this rock pile.

For centuries, native people spent summers along this beach, enjoying many feasts on these tasty mussels. After the meat was eaten, the shells were tossed into a pile. The natives had no garbage service, and after countless years of dining in the same spot and adding to the shell piles, great mounds grew. Today, some of these shell mounds can still be found. But our shell mounds in the Mattole region are really tiny compared to one I read about on the lower Mississippi. It measured five hundred feet in length. However, these natives tossed more into their piles than just shells. Animal, and even human remains were found there. Imagine living back in that time period and having a cranky mother-in-law around. Into the shell mound with her!

Over a hundred years ago a school of Henrietta's ancestors, passing by Mussel Ranch, might have noticed bonfires on the beach. Indians could have been sitting cross-legged enjoying dandelion juice and cooking mussels. Times have changed very little in some ways. In the same spot, a century later, I might have been sitting around such a fire eating mussels and passing around a jug of muscatel.

# 5

# MATTOLE GETS ITS NAME

Two sources of information which I have researched told of the first white men entering Mattole Valley. A local history tells of Alfred Augustus Hadley coming here for a sightseeing trip between 1850 and 1854.

Another book I read on Humboldt County history tells of the John Hill expedition around this same time. When Mr. Hill returned to Fort Humboldt he reported great cattle ranching possibilities in a luscious valley a long day's ride to the south. His proclamation proved prosperous for the early pioneers. These hardy settlers were soon using the word Mattole to describe the whole region surrounding their homesteads.

Mattole is an Indian word meaning clear water. Today if you should look into any of the deep pools along the Mattole River, you will notice the water in the summer is still living up to its Indian title.

# 6

# FROM THE OCEAN TO THE LOWER NORTHFORK

Now it's high time we get into some good ol' Mattole history, and join Henrietta where the big swim begins. It's wintertime now and the Mattole River is swollen bank to bank.

Many coastal streams nearly dry up in late summer. The Mattole is no exception. When the volume of water becomes too little to keep an open channel through the sand dunes at the beach, a battle ensues. The ocean tosses up sand at high tide, and the river cleans it out at low tide. Finally the ocean wins. It builds a sand barrier, and the river backs up behind it and forms a body of water called a lagoon. As long as the river is closed off by this sand barrier, it remains a lagoon. As soon as it opens to the ocean, it's called an estuary. This transformation occurs during the first big storm each autumn, when several inches of rain drench the watershed. At this point, the river rises and regains sufficient force to push against the

*The mouth of the Mattole River forms an estuary when flows are high enough to break through the sand berm that forms between the ocean and the sea.*

sand barrier. This time, the river wins the battle, a new channel is formed, and the fish come rushing in.

In 1885, an early storm deluged the watershed causing the Mattole to rise sufficiently for a huge number of salmon to enter the river on their spawning run. Unfortunately, Mother Nature turned the faucet off abruptly, and stranded the salmon in the lower reaches of the river. The fall drought lasted so long that the river subsided and vast numbers of salmon perished that year.

Shortly after the intrusion of Caucasians to the Mattole, Henrietta's ancestors, resting quietly in the estuary, may have been spooked by a strange phenomenon. It was not unusual for the surface of the estuary to be broken at several places by large splashes from naked bodies sinking down into the chilly winter waters of the estuary.

White settlers brought many gifts to the indigenous people. One of these gifts, they could surely have done without—the measles. When the medicine man dealt with this spotted plague, he believed evil spirits had invaded the stricken members of the tribe. Since there were no aspirin in those times, his cure-all was the sweat lodge. After taking a hot steam bath, the infected ones would run and jump from the bank into the icy waters of the lagoon. During this era of Mattole history, there were around one thousand Indians residing in this area.

There have been many books written regarding the battles between the pioneers and native people. I will not add substantially to these volumes as we are only concerned with landmarks. My analysis of the change in the West from aborigine to newcomer is very short and simple. Our hardy pioneers came traipsing into Mattole Valley bringing fruit trees, guns, and a conquering spirit. They replaced the Indians' food supply with their gardens, corn fields, orchards, and livestock. The natives, having little left to eat, stole beef and vegetables. It's been said that nothing is against the law unless you get caught. When an Indian got caught, he sometimes would get shot. His family would retaliate, and the war was on. When the war was over, all but a few Indians were taken to reservations. Looking back now, it seems a needless expense. Reservations were not really necessary, as I see it. A few more years and the great numbers of white folks moving into Mattole would have taken care of the situation with the new diseases they brought with them: mumps, chicken pox, and smallpox. After a turn in the sweat house, and then hitting the river with a fever, one does not have to be a doctor to prophesy the outcome. Many died from the treatment.

Besides getting one all steamed up, the sweat lodge had other functions. All Indians were taken into the sweat lodge and instructed how to live properly. One of these instructions was to never waste food. Never take more elk, deer or fish than one can eat. When I look around today at my wasteful white brothers, methinks I should build a huge sweat lodge and drag them all into it and give a few lectures as my predecessors received. We do have a tendency to get greedy when fishing or hunting is at its best.

Now we return to our fish friend. One of Hen's ancient relatives had passed along the story of human bodies splashing around in the estuary. At this early point in history it would be easy to identify a tribe by the markings on their bodies. The Mattole Indians used blue marks tattooed on the forehead for males, and three stripes on the chin for females. Today if you sit on the porch of the local store, the only sure way you can tell a real native is by the amount of dust during the summer, or mud during the winter, that is on the Mattolian's vehicle. A clean car, no doubt, would signify a tourist.

If the Indians, swimming in the estuary, didn't spook Henrietta's kinfolks, then the iron horse surely might have. On the north side of the river there once existed a railroad. When the train chugged along to its destination, which was the wharf at the beach, it no doubt shook the mud on the bottom of the lagoon.

*In the early 1900's tanbark was hauled to the commercial wharf at the mouth of the Mattole by horseteam and railroad.*

## COLLINS GULCH

Around 1910, a choo-choo was making regular runs from Petrolia to Collins Point. If you, the reader, are on your toes, you will ask the obvious question. How did Collins Point get its name? Two men from jolly old England owned this land. Their names were George and Joe Collins. The very first tributary of the Mattole that Henrietta passes enters the lagoon from the north slopes. It bears the name of these brothers, and is called Collins Gulch. Even though the Collins brothers owned this property, they lived in Petrolia. Legend has it that they didn't believe in banks, and buried their gold coins somewhere in metropolitan Petrolia.

The railroad and wharf was built by the Stewart family during the tanbark era, but it didn't last much longer than the bark which it transported to waiting ships. Only a few remnants of the tracks are left at the time of this writing, but the old steam engine was restored and moved to McKinleyville in 1956.

*At the tip of the wharf, tanbark was loaded aboard waiting ships bound for San Francisco.*

That's enough rest for Henrietta, and she's eager to move out of the lagoon and proceed up the Mattole.

## BEAR CREEK
After leaving the sea, the second stream we find running into the Mattole is Bear Creek. It enters the

estuary from the south side of the river. Originally it was called Grizzly Creek. The reason for this name is self-explanatory. It was a favorite haunt of the big bear which roamed the entire territory. Besides the fact that bear lived in great numbers along this creek, the tale of an old pioneer who dwelt here makes for a better story. He was not well respected by his neighbors, it seems. Not that he did anything wrong, he just could never relate anything correctly. Each time he was sitting in on a gathering around the potbelly stove at the general store, he would win the liars' contest, even when there was none taking place. Once he was overheard telling a visitor to Petrolia that it hardly ever rained in the Mattole. The visitor remarked that he had heard about a bridge which spanned the Mattole River being washed away during the previous winter. "Well," was the answer, "the durn fog does come in real heavy at times, and when this occurs we lose a bridge now and then."

We just can't leave Bear Creek without a couple more stories. This same untruthful gent told of hunting up the creek one fine day and coming face to face with two enormous grizzlies. There was a big hollow stump right handy, and he jumped into it. He lost his black powder and balls when he went over the edge, and all he had to defend himself with was the one ball and charge already in the weapon. These two giant beasts kept circling round and round the stump, and he knew he had to do something quickly. Laying the rifle over his knee, he bent it into a half circle. He poked it outside and fired. You guessed it! The ball circled around the stump and got both bears! History repeats itself they say, and if you look around it's possible you too may have such a neighbor. This pretentious pioneer had long departed by the time a more respected gentleman appeared on the scene.

Howard Orem, a new property owner on Bear Creek during the 1970's, remembers a mother bear and cub sharing his acreage. There still are bear in the vicinity, and other wildlife too. As a student and lover of nature, Mr. Orem's first days at Bear Creek were spent camping out while he was deciding the proper location to erect a permanent dwelling. He wanted his impact upon the wildlife to be at a minimum.

He pitched two tents near the shelter of a large pepperwood tree. One tent was for sleeping, and one was for provisions. Soon he realized that there were many small four-footed, long-tailed, whiskered residents in close proximity. Their houses were constructed of piles of sticks they collected while out on scavenger hunts. Up until the arrival of the provision tent, these rodents were content with the groceries nature provided them. That soon changed.

After a few petty thefts of food from the tent, it became necessary to store the rations in jars with lids. It wasn't long before the critters learned to wrestle the lids free with their little front feet and enjoy banqueting on the new neighbor's food. Personally, I suspect that this good-natured lover of the outdoors encouraged these antics by tossing meal leftovers to his new found pets.

He tells of one such fearless, four-footed friend that would jump on his sleeping bag each morning at daylight. Upon doing so, the startled sleeper would arise, and soon there would be tasty tidbits forthcoming. Each day his pet would show up and demand its bread ration. The bread supply was kept in what was thought to be a very secure place. It hung from a string tied over the roof pole in the sleeping tent. One morning the string was dangling free, and the bread had vanished. A new loaf was secured to the string, and this time a flashlight lay close at hand. Shortly after dark the next evening came the sound of a rustling bread wrapper. The flashlight illuminated an acrobatic performer hanging from the pole with his back feet, while holding onto the tail of another partner in crime by its front feet. These raids continued, and extended to other provisions as well. Several empty glass containers had disappeared from the cache, and that was all right, but shortly thereafter, a few full beverage bottles vanished too. Now it was definitely time to commence building a house, and you can bet your boots, it was rat-proof.

## STANSBERRY CREEK

Less than a mile and a half from the ocean, a little creek enters the Mattole from the southwest. Henrietta's spawning run nearly stopped here, due to the fact that my work on this book almost ended at this point. I wrote letters, made phone calls, and studied old documents with no success.

Eventually, I found an 1865 map with the name of Francis Stansberry in this area. The Stansberry name definitely had roots here, validating the origin of the creek's name. Both Hen and I were satisfied enough with this information to continue on up the river.

## PROSPER RIDGE

Prosper Ridge is the headwater ridge of Stansberry Creek. As I queried old-timers about the origin of Prosper, I received various answers. When I spoke with a local shepherd, I told him I was given an idea of someone living up there and becoming prosperous. He snorted and said, "The only prosperity gained in those hills was by the coyotes." It seems he had driven a large flock of sheep to this area and the coyotes had dined upon many of them.

While checking out various records and visiting tombstones I located the name Prosper and was sure I had gained the answer. However, I learned of another Prosper, and even though it was his first name and not last name, old-timers guaranteed me that I would not go wrong by confirming the title for Prosper Bigot. It was he who inhabited Prosper Ridge.

## MOORE HILL

Let's switch to the north side of the Mattole now. The 1860 census shows John Moore residing there as a farmer. An 1866 map reveals no more Moore. In this era, because of the Indian troubles, many settlers left rather suddenly for parts unknown.

## RACKLIFF HOLE

The Rackliff Hole is one fishing spot I'll never forget. It is impossible for anyone to keep an accurate record of the river as it meanders each winter in the stretch between the George Lindley bridge and the lagoon. Mother Nature liked to play games with the hydrology, making this stretch of river a mapmaker's nightmare.

Once the Mattole meandered north until it created a very deep and long pool by the edge of Moore Hill. This excellent fishing spot derived its name from the man owning land there—Clark Rackliff.

One winter this hole became so shallow at the upper end that the fish could not traverse it; thus, they were blocked for days from going further. Each day new runs of steelhead would come in from the ocean and be trapped there. When I learned of this situation, a friend and I cut school and went to have a look. We climbed trees and tossed small rocks down into the hole. A huge black mass of fish could be seen moving around. We could only estimate the number. It was in the thousands. Being poor and owning no poles or tackle, we borrowed line and hooks, tied rocks on for sinkers, and heaved the tackle as far out into the pool as we could. We landed several steelies in this manner. We were but a few fishermen casting into a mass of thousands of steelhead. Today, it's quite the opposite. Thousands of fishermen toss fancy tackle into pools with very few fish.

Just a stone's toss above this great fishing hole was a sort of island that Mattole residents called Ball Flat. Walter Ball lived here.

Another Ball, whom I located in research, was J. Ball. He was a member of the first Grange organized in Petrolia in 1874.

A story which is slightly humorous concerns a gentleman also living in this area who supposedly owned a team of deaf animals. Each morning that he hitched up his team, he would yell at them so loudly that neighbors could hear him bawling at the animals almost to Petrolia. Consequently, this story of Bawl Flat evolved. This spot is a shining example of how history slips away. Today, you can hardly find anyone under the age of seventy that remembers Ball Flat.

## JIM GOFF GULCH

Moving upstream now, we come to a very small rivulet which drains Jim Goff Gulch. This little stream holds no interest for our Henrietta, but it does bring to mind some history regarding the Goff family.

Stephen Goff came from North Carolina to Mattole in 1859. He was Jim Goff's father. In the book *Regional History of Petrolia and the Lower Mattole Valley*, T.K. Clark tells of Mr. Goff's treks to town, where Jim would stand on the bar in a saloon and wave his hat and proclaim in a loud voice, "Mattole Against the World!" There have been times that I have witnessed some Mattolians draped over a bar alright, but I've never noticed such a display of patriotism as that performed by Mr. Goff.

## UNCLE TOMMY

As the river meanders, so shall we. Switching back to the south shore, let us take our story up into the hills to a mountain peak known as Uncle Tommy. There were two Tom Scotts, I found, owning land in the Mattole. One was an oil man from the East, and the other man was of Indian descent. One Scott, I know not which, owned 320 acres near the area called Uncle Tommy.

The Petrolia Precinct Register of Voters from the year 1896 showed Thomas Scott, a thirty-one-year-old laborer, with dark complexion, dark color of eyes, black hair, and a scar on his forehead, registered as a native of California. In addition, it was noted that he was unable to read the Constitution in the English language, and was unable to write his name. Obviously, this was the Indian Tom Scott.

Because the Petrolia oil boom was a bust by 1896, the oil man Scott, not listed on the voter register of that time, had already departed for more lucrative diggings.

The Indian Scott and his family once lived on the south side of the river but had to do their shopping on the north side because that was where the store was located. Often it became necessary, when the river was swollen, to use a boat to shop. Mr. Scott had a very lovely daughter, and one fine day she needed a ride in a boat to reach the store. A young man residing along the Mattole offered her his services as boatman, which she graciously accepted. Had one of Henrietta's ancestors been swimming along under this boat she would have been spooked by the antics of the craft. She could have encountered many rowboats in her swim upstream by now, but surely never one that behaved as this boat did. The story goes like this. The oarsman demanded the sweet miss in the stern to surrender all her charms or learn to swim at once. With this, he began to rock the boat to and fro, but overdid it and both went swimming. No doubt about it, the cold water cooled off his passion immediately. So much for his romance on the Mattole.

## MILL CREEK

Henrietta's ancestors may have gotten sawdust in their eyes near the mouth of this creek. The origin of the name Mill Creek, located on the south side, was easy to determine. Early in Mattole's history, equipment was freighted into the valley. Mills were set up and the business of lumber-making began.

George Hill had a sawmill at this location as early as 1865. It was water powered, and due to his ability in turning big trees into lumber, he furnished boards for many of the original Petrolia homes. Another operator of this sawmill was Bill Erwin. Mr. Erwin was one of many folks to lose their lives in the Mattole. He was attempting to cross the river one night on horseback and was never seen again. Since the horse couldn't talk, it was never known if he fell in or met with foul play. In the Petrolia cemetery there is an unusual marker which reads: "Lost Brother Bill." It was erected by his sisters.

A good reason for Henrietta's big-nosed ancestors to avoid the mouth of this creek was the occasional milling of white fir. The odor of white fir is generally described by a word I hesitate to print here. I can only say it reminds me of a neighbor I once had who owned twenty-seven cats. The waft of air from their litter box would automatically wrinkle your nose long before you reached the house. Fortunately, the mill is long gone, and now salmon have the opportunity to enjoy the clean, clear waters of Mill Creek.

## TOM SCOTT CREEK

There is very little about the life of Mr. Scott that I can add here which has not already been mentioned earlier during the Uncle Tommy discussion. This little creek entering the Mattole near Evergreen Way, on the southwest side, obviously was named for Tom Scott, but whether it was the oilman or Indian is unclear. I think it was probably the Indian.

## TITUS CREEK

This creek is in the same proximity as Tom Scott Creek. They're only a stone's throw from each other. I hadn't come across Titus Creek named on any maps, and I nearly left it out. Shame on me had I done so, because the name is famous and has been around for a long time. Titus was the emperor of Rome in the year 80 A.D., but this creek here in the Mattole wasn't named for him. In 1866, George Moore Gary Titus and his family came to the lower Mattole Valley as some of the first pioneers. It was probably named for them. Fayette Titus is the one I remember residing at this location. Descendants of this family still have holdings in Petrolia. I was reminded of this name by talking with the local neighbors, and by seeing that the Humboldt County Assessor's Office maps refer to this creek as such.

It is interesting to note that the first oil well drilled in the United States was in 1859 at Titusville, Pennsylvania. The Tituses were also here during the oil boom in Petrolia, the site of the first oil well to be drilled in California. I am sure there is no connection, and it is strictly a coincidence, but the Titus name seems to pop up where the action is.

## JEFFRY GULCH
Returning to the north bank of the river, there is a drainage known as Jeffry Gulch. It was named for Jim Jeffry who owned land here in 1865.

## LOWER NORTHFORK
Remaining on the north side now, we come to the history surrounding the Lower Northfork of the Mattole River. If Henrietta or any of her thousands of relatives had been born here, they would diverge from the main river and take up residence in many of the deep holes of the Lower Northfork.

Once upon a time the cold waters of this creek provided excellent spawning grounds for salmon. To prove to you that fish lived in the Lower Northfork by large numbers, I must stop here and relate an interesting happening. A local rancher, riding horseback down the creek one day, let his horse have free reign. The animal was thirsty, and wading cinch deep into a pool, began to slurp the clear water of the Lower Northfork. Several salmon resting in this same pool looked up and their eyes were confronted by this large, hairy beast invading their tranquility. These fish had encountered hungry sea lions in the ocean, but never before a beast this large. They didn't bother to check out the caliber of the enemy, but turned tail and fled down the creek. Passing the next pool they spooked a few more resting spawners, and these fish sensed the fear of their shiny counterparts and also took to flight. Pool after pool went the splashing throng, and each one added to the wave of terror. The horse and rider sat in utter consternation, neither realizing for a few minutes what had taken place. Downstream nearly a quarter of a mile away, spray from the pounding tails of untold fleeing salmon could still be witnessed. This story indicates that the Lower Northfork at one time hosted a large population of fish.

## YELLOW ROSE

Where the Petrolia road crosses the Lower Northfork there is a small bridge. The building sitting near the bridge on the town side, is the Yellow Rose — a place where one can buy food and drink. I was told the Rose was just a name chosen right out of the blue, and holds no history. However, I must interject a pair of stories regarding this establishment.

When speaking of weather, there's an old saying that history repeats itself every one hundred years. Well, the site of the Yellow Rose is living proof that it didn't happen here. When talking with Fred Farnsworth, he told me about his folks living near this spot around 1886. Their home was washed away by a disastrous flood caused by too much snow in the hills which melted from heavy, warm rains, causing the Lower Northfork to become nearly as large as the Mattole River itself.

A tale on the lighter side now. In the spring of 1981, I was passing through Petrolia with a friend and her four-year-old daughter. I was calling out the names of places, as it was their first trip into the Mattole. The little girl asked about the Rose. I told her we might stop there and have a drink and a hamburger if we had time, and that's what most do there at that place. On the way back we found a herd of cows wandering down the middle of the county road just before we reached the cafe. Abruptly the bovines turned into the parking lot and went around back looking for the creek. When I mentioned that the cows were probably going for a drink, the little girl's eyes popped wide and she whirled around to her mother and asked, "Are they going to have hamburgers too?"

While on the subject of cows, I might mention that I came across an old ledger dating back to 1891. A cow was worth twenty dollars then. Last week I paid thirteen dollars for a bale of alfalfa and it didn't last my cow a week! Talk about inflation.

## CREAMERY HILL

Crossing the little bridge by the Yellow Rose and traveling westward, you soon climb Creamery Hill. All through childhood I never knew why it was thus named. One day we gave a ride to an old pioneer by the name of Sam Kelsey. He was just short of one hundred years young. He pointed out the location where Mr. Glass once built a creamery in 1891. The milk was sledded up Creamery Hill to the plant where it was made into butter. Among other places, this butter was hauled by pack animals to the gold fields near Weaverville some 150 miles away.

The creamery was located across the county road from the eucalyptus trees which grow along the roadside. These trees were planted by a man known quite well in Humboldt history, Mr. Jack Smiley, a distant relative of mine in fact. Smiley had the longest name in the English language. There was a mile between the first and last letters.

On the northwest side of the eucalyptus trees was

the racetrack. Horse racing was a prime attraction for the early pioneers. Across the road from the racetrack once stood one of Petrolia's first hotels, in operation in 1866. H. Anderson was the proprietor, and it was called the Table Hotel. This location is still referred to as The Table.

## GRIZZLY CREEK

Returning to the Lower Northfork now, I would like to mention a few of its tributaries. The first one that we come to, which runs north/south, is called Grizzly Creek. Bear existed extensively here. In fact, one man met a giant grizzly while hunting in the nearby area now known as Joel Flat. Joel Benton went squirrel hunting here armed only with a small caliber rifle. Rounding a big rock, he came nose to nose with this giant. Be honest readers, what would you have done? He ran so fast, it is told, that he beat his shadow back to Petrolia. Later, when anyone from Petrolia would mention a planned trip anywhere near this location, someone would grin and say, take care up there on Joel Flat!

Joel Benton came here in 1857. He was noted as a pacifist. He attempted to make peace between Indians and white men. But, when he dealt with the grizzly, he met with defeat. No such word as arbitration was in the bear's vocabulary.

Around 1860 there were a half dozen other Joels in the territory. By 1865, even another Joel popped up in this land of opportunity. J. Henderson, a prominent citizen of Petrolia, in a newspaper article at that time wrote that the boring of the oil well on Joel Rush Flat was proceeding rapidly. I have found no other mention of Mr. Rush in my research, but I am satisfied that the name Joel Flat was handed down as a result of his stay on the Lower Northfork.

## JOEL FLAT CREEK

There is a Joel Flat Creek, which is separated by Farnsworth Ridge from Grizzly Creek. Fred Farnsworth told me that his folks had moved to this location after they had been flooded out on the Lower Northfork. The first Farnsworth to enter the Mattole Valley came here from Wisconsin. Fred told me that his grandfather (also named Fred) had walked every step of the way to California in 1858 herding stock. Each time I pass the Petrolia cemetery, I take my hat off to that hardy pioneer. Recently, I walked seven miles from my home to the Petrolia store for a few groceries. Painfully, I had only five mile feet.

It was also a Farnsworth who freighted the first thrashing machine into the Mattole Valley. This preceding fact is historical as well as humorous, because as a small lad, when I heard folks speak of the Brown thrasher I always thought it was some type of rare bird. My head was so thick you couldn't stir it with a stick. When doing research for this book, I read where Mr. Brown in Ferndale had owned the first thrasher. (Actually I shouldn't have mentioned this in the book, because now it may get listed as an endangered species.)

Not far from here I've heard rumors there's a pretty little valley that is tucked away so nicely I've never found it! That must be why it's called Hidden

Valley. I understand that it once was known as Gun Valley, and in those days maybe some folks wished it had been more hidden.

Many families have dwelt along the Lower Northfork, and some early maps and records refer to a name that made history. That name was John Barkdull, and he came to California in 1860. He was the scout who saved the Eli Bagley wagon train. John married Nancy Bagley. One of their four children was believed to be the first white child born south of Cape Mendocino in the Mattole Valley area. The infant was named Mendocino. Mr. Bagley first settled in the vicinity of Stansberry Creek. He planted many acres of English walnuts along the Mattole in his farming career.

Moving on up the Lower Northfork there were two Scottish gentlemen who owned a large ranch. They introduced the use of dogs to the growing cattle business. These men, George and Donald Edmondston, very soon had many other ranchers training dogs, and even today dogs are still found to be useful when gathering stock.

Included in their extensive land holdings is property known as the Paragon. This is a grassy prairie that can be seen when looking southward from Taylor Peak. Try as I might, I could find no logical reason for this name. Finally, I learned that there was a ship named the *Paragon* making regular voyages into Humboldt Bay in the early 1800's. My simple mind told me that it was quite possible they traveled on this vessel. Unfortunately, this ship was also registered as a marine disaster at the Crescent City harbor in March of 1850. This was well before the Edmondstons arrived in the Mattole, and left me once again without an explanation. A few weeks before this book went to press, I was perusing a handful of newspaper clippings collected by Lyn Chambers. Lo and behold, the Paragon was the name of an oil well located along the Lower Northfork in the appropriate location to receive the final honors.

Much of the water in the Lower Northfork drains from the area around the East Fork. The East Branch of the Lower Northfork originates at Sulphur Creek. Sulphur Creek, in turn, originates near the backbone of Rainbow Ridge. What is interesting about this situation is the fact that the beginning of Upper Northfork is just over the ridge about a quarter mile away. A winter raindrop falling in this location has a decision to make. If it falls slightly on the south side of Little Rainbow Ridge, which separates the two northforks, then it ends up flowing down the Upper Northfork. However, if it falls slightly on the north side of Little Rainbow Ridge, it joins the waters of the Lower Northfork. Decisions, decisions, decisions. I'm happy I'm not a raindrop!

There is one tributary to the Lower Northfork, the title of which is unprintable. Mapmakers did not print it even though many old-timers know the name of this little stream. My source of the story related the following. A man living by this creek was very inventive. He erected his outhouse over the stream. When Mother Nature called him for a trip to the little shed, and he used it, the creek did the flushing. Folks living downstream, needing a drink, or collecting wash water, gave vent to their feelings by giving this little creek its unprintable name.

## HORNBACK

Overlooking the junction of Burnt Ranch Creek with the Lower Northfork is Hornback Ridge. This was named for Anthony Hornback who lived there, according to the 1860 census.

In 1864 Hornback Peak became one of the boundaries for the new Mattole oil district.

## TAYLOR PEAK

One of my ancestors — Cyrus Miner — lived on the Lower Northfork. Like many of us Miners he did nothing very famous for me to write about. He just lived on the East Branch and enjoyed life. Looking back though, just existing in those early times was a great feat. What with grizzlies, Indians on the warpath, and rattlesnakes, just to stay alive was an accomplishment.

I went to Cyrus's homestead once when I was a youngster. Fishing was fantastic. At that time there was a massive logjam at this location and the trout had a great hiding place underneath it. There were two routes around this pile of logs and brush; a very steep shale slide on one end, and Taylor Peak on the other. The mountain reaches into the sky 3,374 feet. Needless to say, I didn't choose to climb that high. I talked with so many old-timers concerning the origin of the name of this towering peak that I can't remember them all. I always came away from these many conversations with no reason for the Taylor title. Finally, in desperation, I went to Western Title Company and prevailed on their good nature to do some checking. Bingo! There was a Moses Taylor living there in 1904. Moses did not live on top of the peak itself, but down on the Lower Northfork. Most pioneers lived near water, and this seemed like a good plan to me—live by the creek, yet have the mountain named for you.

Jim Cook, whose family once owned much of this watershed, told me of another Taylor living nearby who was a woodcutter. There are a few folks who remember this spot also. It is near the old road which once ran along the creek itself. It is referred to as Taylor's Flat, and is not to be mistaken for the rancho of Moses Taylor.

Another one of my ancestors, Cyrus Miner's brother Jacob, also lived on Taylor's Peak. This land has changed hands several times, and yet it is still referred to as the Miner.

## SHUMAKER RIDGE

Up on the side of Taylor Peak is Shumaker Ridge. G.E. Shumaker lived here in 1869. Remnants still remain of an old stove he once used. They just don't make stoves like that anymore! I ran across a clipping from an old paper which told of Mr. Shumaker having operated a store of some kind in Petrolia. When I first heard of his name, I jumped to the conclusion that he must have lived on the side of the peak and made shoes. This is what I get for thinking for myself and not sticking to hard facts. Eventually I learned from another old clipping that Mr. Shumaker was the very first clerk of the very first store in Petrolia.

Do you have a neighbor who jumps into his car and drives to the store a half mile away for a pound of butter? The following is a shining example of just how soft we have become. Over 125 years ago, butter was made in the Petrolia area, and transported the hard way. Some of the early residents up the Lower Northfork had dairies—the Weeks family for one. Maggie Weeks was a daughter of Moses Conklin, whom we will discuss in a few pages. The Edmondstons also had a dairy business in what is called Edmondston Gulch. These hardy folks would milk cows, then churn and pack butter into containers, which were placed in the cold ground. In the spring, the butter would be packed by mules to Port Kenyon and loaded on ships. As I mentioned, some of it even found its way to the gold fields near Redding. What a difference today, when you can drive to the store anytime you want, and grab a pound from the freezer!

## BURNT RANCH

The main stream of the Lower Northfork watershed follows the west side of Taylor Peak. Some people refer to this section of the stream as Burnt Ranch Creek. I don't have enough fingers or toes to count the number of older folks I have queried about this place. Finally, I received a card from Bob Morrison at Bear River. His uncle, Silas Morrison, once owned this land. It was called Burnt Ranch as far back as one hundred years ago. It was extremely brushy acreage and it required frequent burning to keep the land clear for grazing. People riding through would remember it as the Burnt Ranch.

## WALKER MOUNTAIN
Between Taylor Peak and the Pacific Ocean is Walker Mountain, which reaches a height of 2,654 feet. It was Jesse and John Walker that the mountain was named for, although others may have lived there first.

You may notice that I don't mention a few names that do appear on some maps such as Long Ridge, or Brushy Ridge. These I feel are self-explanatory, so I won't take up space with them.

One more paragraph about the Walker name before we leave this part of the world. It concerns Jesse Walker. An old clipping I found tells of his interest in politics. Once there was a community picnic grounds a short distance up the Lower Northfork from the existing county road. Jesse Walker was in charge of refreshments there when Petrolia had a big celebration as a result of an honor bestowed upon the voters in this area. This tiny village had turned out the most Republican votes for a town its size. Today there would be something to celebrate if fifty percent of the public turned out to vote. How times change, huh?

## FRUIT RANCH
One more name along the Lower Northfork, which is very unusual, is Fruet. John and Israel Fruit owned property far up on the west branch of the Lower Northfork. Now you might accuse me of typing poorly as I spell this name. Once I have spelled the name Fruet, and then again Fruit. There is an old history I have read that tells of the Fruet brothers coming to the Mattole country in 1857. That history

spelled the name with "et." Maps and other notes of historical interest show the correct spelling as "it." John and Israel, I really must apologize, for I am darned if I know yet which spelling is proper to use. But, they left behind a landmark called the Fruit Ranch, and it's not what one might think when hearing the name for the first time. It was not because there were large stands of fruit trees there. They might have been Fruet trees, however.

This is enough for the Lower Northfork. Let's rejoin Henrietta in the Mattole River. As we return to the river proper, you might wonder why Henrietta didn't take this side trip with us. There are two reasons. One reason is because of the bad floods this region experienced in 1955 and also in 1964. Most of the deep holes, where fish would rest while on their spawning run, were nearly filled with gravel and soil deposited by the severe flooding. The other reason is not so disastrous, but actually is humorous. For the sake of argument (and it's doubtless any reader will challenge my theory), let's say that fish have a method of communicating. Try to imagine the story handed down to Henrietta by one of her ancestors who was frightened by the previously mentioned monster somewhere along the canyon of the Lower Northfork. Whatever the reason, floods or monsters, most salmon have bypassed the Lower Northfork in recent years.

# 7

# PETROLIA

## THE TOWN

If you are a resident of Petrolia, or you once were a dweller of this little village, then I have a tidbit of information just for you. Have you ever been unhappy with the way the streets and town sites were laid out? Or, possibly you are pleased with them. Whichever way you feel, I can tell you who did the planning for Petrolia. Their names were J.S. Murray, J. Henderson, and M.J. Conklin. If you are a stranger to Petrolia, and ever get lost on the streets of this giant metropolis, you now know who to blame.

In 1864, an early pioneer named John McAuliffe, living on the lower Mattole, won a contest for his choice of a name for the new settlement. His choice was Petroleum. Later research uncovered the fact that Mr. Henderson, another resident of the community, decided a more appropriate name would be Petrolia. The seed was planted for this idea by Mr. McAuliffe, and I am willing to see him get full credit and honors.

The first "store" to do business in Petrolia was situated in a log building with planks across a couple of barrels. That was in 1864. That same year, twenty-

*An aerial view shows the little village of Petrolia with the Mattole River in the background meandering past Moore Hill and on toward the ocean.*

five-year-old Darlington J. Johnson from Pennsylvania chanced to read a newspaper story about the discovery of oil in the Mattole area. "Ten barrels a day," the story read. He hitched his team to the wagon, and soon came to see the oil fields for himself. The oil boom was a bust. D. J. Johnson diversified into general merchandising and became proprietor for another store in Petrolia. This should teach us not to believe everything we see in the papers! It is now over 120 years since D. J. Johnson pulled his team and wagon to a halt in Petrolia, and we are still looking for the eleventh barrel!

Some oil stock sold for five hundred dollars per share. During the influx of speculators to the new oil community, the perceived prosperity produced new hotels, stores, saloons, and even a library, but it seems there was little money for investing in bank accounts. At five hundred dollars a share for worthless stock, I can see why.

Let me interject right here that I was concerned as to what designation I should give Petrolia. Should I refer to it as a village or a town? Consulting my *Funk and Wagnalls,* I found that the definition of a town is described as being larger than a village and also could be a group of prairie-dog burrows. There are lots of gopher holes around Petrolia, and I find myself wondering if these would suffice to title it a town.

By 1860 there were 282 residents around Petrolia. In the early nineteen hundreds the population topped out at 675. Then by 1950 it had fallen down to 361.

Before I leave the subject of stores, I find I cannot restrain myself from interjecting another one of my fascinating thoughts. In 1858, there was a treaty drawn up between the Indians and the white settlers. This document specified that no red man should eat any of the white man's cows, or trespass into any planted fields or gardens. This left the Indian between a rock and a hard place, so to speak. The pioneers with their fire sticks had eliminated nearly all of the deer and elk herds. Consequently, the Indian had no place to shop for his supper.

At this point in the Mattole's history, it seems to me, the Indians missed a golden opportunity to change history. If they had erected a trading post in downtown Petrolia and put up a big sign on it that read: "INDIANS ONLY, NO WHITES PERMITTED," history could have taken a decisive turn in a new direction.

As trees grow, and later fall, and new trees take their place, so too have many buildings come and gone in Petrolia. I will not try to relate to you each and every old saloon, store, school, or hotel which has at one time or another existed. However, I will mention a few which are notable.

Overlooking the town is the Catholic church. Its construction was financed by Patrick Mackey. Later in 1910, it was dedicated in his memory by his widow.

I remember quite well a severe electric storm Petrolia experienced one winter. A bolt of lightning struck the steeple of this church and did extensive damage. When I arrived on the scene, there was a small crowd of residents looking at the destruction. I still smile when I think of a comment made by one of the local citizens. Mr. "B" turned to me with a big grin and said, "I wonder which one of them folks did something wrong last week?"

If you were to walk out to the edge of the road in front of the Catholic church and gaze thoughtfully at the land below, you may imagine an old building which once stood there. This tiny building once housed the first phone company in our town, and later also served as the post office. The first post office was called Mattole. Delivery of mail into the Mattole began as early as 1863, and by 1890 had been increased from twice a week to six days a week. Personally, I wish deliveries were seven days a week. That way I'd have junk mail and bills to start my wood fired heater on Sunday, too.

If oil had been found in larger quantities, then and only then, a much larger building may have been built for the volumes of mail, and thousands of phones that would have been here. Our town may have been named Petroliapolis instead.

I was speaking of telephones, but my thoughts got disconnected. At one time in our phone history there were nearly thirty phones connected to just one pair of wires running the entire length of the valley. Each party had its own ring. I remember that on our ranch it was two long rings, and three short ones. When our bell rang, this meant twenty-nine other phones along the line heard our ring also. If your wife, or even your horse, was to give birth soon, the approaching event was common knowledge. When your phone would jingle, you could soon hear many clicks of other receivers being picked up off their hooks also. As each receiver was lifted, the signal would become weaker and weaker, until you could hardly hear the party who called you. This act of eavesdropping was called rubbering, which was possibly derived from the term rubbernecking. The year 1915 was a great year for Mattole. One could now call all the way to Eureka and points beyond.

In 1903 Petrolia was nearly wiped out by a wildfire. A fire district was formed in 1951, and I am happy to be living in this part of the century. We won't have a repeat of such a disaster with a modern fire department. However, in April of 1992, a vicious earthquake shook Petrolia and caused the General Store to burn down. Local fire department volunteers were 150 miles away attending a stress conference. Back in Petrolia the fire laddies in town were living real stressful moments. The roll-up door at the fire station jammed shut from the quake, and the Petrolia Volunteer Fire Department was temporarily inoperative. We lost the post office also; but it was April and the grass was green, so the fire spread no further and history did not repeat itself.

Across the highway from the rebuilt General Store is a plaque commemorating the first oil well drilled in California. In 1865/66 the first shipment of oil left Petrolia for San Francisco. Large heavy blankets were saturated in oil, then rolled up in tight bundles and hauled out on muleback. Later the oil was squeezed from the blankets in order to retrieve it. Since that date much more oil has been shipped in than ever shipped out. There is a picture hanging on the wall in a home in Petrolia showing a ten-mule team dragging a wagonload of oil containers bound for San Francisco. At that market it would fetch $1.40 a gallon. Last week I paid $1.40 a quart for oil.

Let's bring back the mules!

For San Francisco to get the oil, there had to be seaworthy ships available. There was a schooner named *Petrolia* built in 1866. The vision must have been for it to haul thousands of gallons of oil, but because the oil was not forthcoming, it turned to hauling lumber instead, about 65,000 linear feet per load.

I won't try to tell you of the numerous oil wells which have been drilled since the very first one, as this information would be sufficient to write an enormous book. I will go so far as to say that if all the oil casing sunk in Mattole's oil fields was laid end to end, it just might reach some spot where there is actually some oil.

Many churches in Petrolia were formed and later disbanded. However, the Adventist Church, built in 1882, is still active.

Another building erected in 1882 is the home between the school house and the Catholic Church. One of my ancestors — Jacob Miner — hammered it together.

Speaking of the school, let me refer you to a book written by the teachers and students of the Petrolia school in 1962. Its title is *The Book of Petrolia,* and it is a very indepth story of local history.

In 1907, a large structure was built on the present schoolyard. It replaced the schoolhouse near the site of the Yellow Rose which was severely damaged by the 1906 earthquake. Eventually, the newer building was moved across the street from the schoolyard, and now serves as the Mattole Valley Community Center.

I attended classes in this old building and there is

one incident which is too good to keep to myself. I returned to my desk one lunchtime a little early. I had hardly gotten settled when there was a loud yell and crash in the supply room directly ahead of my desk. Two brothers (whose names must remain anonymous) went tearing out the door and ran outside. Inside the supply room things were strewn around, and one might think the 1906 earthquake had struck again. Later I learned what had taken place. One of these boys, while looking for certain supplies, heard a noise overhead in the large attic. He climbed the ladder, opened the trap door, and peered into the attic. He was so astounded that he called his brother to climb up and look. It seems that a few of the lovely young ladies decided to have a beauty contest during the lunch hour. They were parading back and forth in their nothingness. The top brother on the ladder had never seen so much bare skin before, and in his amazement forgot to hang onto the top rung. He fell back, taking his brother with him. They grabbed at shelves on their way down, cleaning most of the supplies from them. No, I never did find out who won the contest.

## CRANE HILL

It's best we leave the school now, after that story, and travel in a southerly direction. The road starts down a short incline known as Crane Hill. I ascended this hill each day on the school bus, but few cranes were to be seen. When I researched this area, I found that Charles Crane once lived in this neighborhood. It is definite that he was the source of the title, and not the great blue herons that I occasionally witnessed. He was a horse lover and had a fast runner he raced on the track behind the eucalyptus trees on the Table.

An old clipping I found told of Mrs. Crane's brother, Tom Stewart, once operating the Capetown Hotel. I confirmed this with Prescott Branstetter.

# 8

# LINDLEY BRIDGE TO LINDLEY BRIDGE

### GEORGE LINDLEY BRIDGE

It's high time we got back to the river and followed Henrietta's wake upstream. It goes without saying that the only way our imaginary salmon could ever witness any of the previously mentioned landmarks would be in some citizen's pocket as a hunk of smoked fish.

After Crane Hill, we cross the flat and arrive at the George Custer Lindley Bridge. Mr. Lindley was born locally on Green Ridge in 1882. He spent his entire life here as a rancher and county supervisor. His long service to the people as a supervisor was eventually rewarded by the dedication of this bridge in his name. You might wonder why I have included the picture of a modern bridge in this book about historical roots. My reasoning is very simple. Shortly after this bridge was opened to traffic, a

*The George Custer Lindley Bridge is a veteran of both floods and earthquakes.*

winter flood washed out the north approach, nearly ruining its chances of ever becoming an old bridge. Then, in April, 1992, a series of three earthquakes occurred within a twenty-four hour period. They ranged from 6.6 to over 7 in magnitude. Again the bridge required major repairs. I have attempted to include only older history in these pages; however, it is my sincere hope that this book will be on library shelves for the next hundred years or so, and considering the calamities wreaked upon the bridge during its early existence, I thought it might be wise to have a picture of it in case the third time around proved fatal.

    A few miles south of this bridge on the south side of Shenanigan Ridge, you will cross another bridge.

This is the Elwyn Lindley Bridge. He was also a supervisor for Humboldt County, and was the eldest son of George Lindley.

## THE HIDEAWAY

At the north end of the George Lindley Bridge stands a metal building. Originally, it was erected for use as a garage by John Lyman. Later he converted it into a bar. This building, known as "The Hideaway," does not go back very far in history, but a very funny incident took place here one night which was related to me by one of its earlier proprietors, and I will share it with you. It might brighten up an otherwise dull page.

A few thirsty patrons were imbibing one evening, when a discussion began involving false teeth. One customer amazed everyone present by stating that he had owned false teeth for many years. He proved it by removing them and setting them on the bar. Another customer, not wishing to be outdone, took his out and laid them on the bar also. The game, whatever it was, caught on like wildfire, and soon there were nearly a dozen sets of ivories on the bar grinning back at the participants. The bartender had a wild sense of humor, and not wanting to be left out of the game, swept all of the dentistry into a big pile with his bar rag. Entertainment comes in unusual forms in the Mattole, but I think tickets could have been sold at a premium price to watch that show. Just imagine each participant trying every set of choppers until they found their individual dentures! The club has changed hands several times since, but the bartender who piled up the grinders is no doubt still smiling somewhere.

Very recently, I had a short visit with Doris Myers—a former owner of The Hideaway. I learned that she was the one who named that establishment, and why. It seems that many folks used to refer to this metal building as the Tin Can. This description did not add much dignity to the business. The building was hard to locate, and because of the type of structure, didn't look like a bar. The name Hideaway seemed fitting and proper.

One patron must have taken exception to the neon sign Doris installed advertising the new name. After popping a few tabs of his favorite brew, he no doubt thought that "The Race Track" would be a better name. He went out the door and came back in on his motorcycle! After rearing the bike on its haunches and doing a few wheelies around the bar's interior, he suddenly gave up the idea. He was now more concerned with a quick exit, as the irate lady was pursuing him with a cleaver. Rifles, pistols, bull whips, and knives were a few of the weapons which tamed the West. Now we have just added a new one: a meat cleaver. It was this clever cleaver which helped, no doubt, to make The Hideaway the peaceful place that it is today.

## EAST MILL CREEK

Moving upstream a short way we come to East Mill Creek. Mr. James Newton Dudley once operated a lumber mill here. Also, further up this creek, Mr. Langdon had a grist mill. There is a book, entitled *The Dudley Family of Iowa*, that tells of a tragedy which took place at this lumber mill. One of my ancestors drowned at this location in April, 1886. The details of his demise are fully chronicled in that book, written by Denis Edeline.

## APPLE TREE RIDGE
Much of the water in East Mill Creek descends from Apple Tree Ridge. I spoke with an old-timer in his nineties concerning this name. He told me he had ridden up this ridge when he was a very small boy. He remembered quite well that one lonely apple tree grew along the trail which traversed the ridge, hence that title.

## CADY RIDGE
Additional water feeds into East Mill Creek from a ridge named Cady. In 1867, Charles Cady was listed on the voter's registration roster for Petrolia. Additionally, an 1898 map showed an E. Cady pioneering that ridge. There are no Cadys residing here today, but the name remains. In this book you will notice that this is so often the case. No matter how many folks have lived on property since the first settlers, it still bears the name of the first family to have lived there.

 A descendant of the original Mattole Indians told me about some great fires in their history of the valley. It seems they burned off the entire valley each year in order to starve out the vast elk herds which grazed here. The animals would have to migrate to the coast to find food, and in doing so, would have to enter a narrow pass. Here the Indians would lie in wait with bows and arrows. The meat would be jerked or smoked, the hides tanned, and even the bones had some usage.

In l964 high up on this ridge a match was dropped by a local rancher. A controlled burn was the order of the day; however, Mother Nature had other plans. A strong wind sprang up and the fire got away. It soon had eaten its way nearly to Honeydew and all the way to the ocean. No buildings of consequence were lost, and no lives. Only lots of dead limbs, underbrush, and old grass were consumed for the most part. Overall, it did more good than harm. I remember a comment from one of the local citizens when the fire was finally corralled. He looked around the valley and said, "The Indians couldn't have done better."

Our Henrietta, approaching the mouth of East Mill Creek, is lucky not to have encountered a strange animal swimming up to her. A few years ago, in the early l980's, a driving rainstorm caused this creek to rise extremely high. When a herd of cows attempted to cross the swollen stream, all made it with the exception of one young heifer. She was swept down the creek and under the road through the huge metal culvert. If fish and bovine met eyeball to eyeball out there in the middle of the Mattole, it's hard to guess who would have been more astounded. As this young bovine staggered out onto the bank of the river, she would have a strange tale to relate to her cousin cows—that is if cows do such things as tell tall tales.

## CLEAR CREEK

Switching to the opposite side of the Mattole, we now find Henrietta resting at the mouth of Clear

Creek. It gets this name because of the fact that it hardly ever becomes muddy.

One day some small fingerlings were startled to see two humans floating along in the river near this area. Tragedy befell Donald Roberts and his son. Both drowned while attempting to cross the river. A very strange coincidence regarding these fatalities is that Mr. Roberts' brother and father had also drowned. They lost their lives at sea, and thirty-five years later the above-mentioned father perished in the Mattole.

Upon leaving the area around Clear Creek, some of Hen's ancestors may have been spooked by one of the largest splashes ever to be heard along the Mattole River. During the peak of the logging boom in the valley, a loaded logging truck was crossing a bridge at this spot when the bridge collapsed. The truck and driver both went into the river with the bridge. The logger was in a hurry to get home for something special, but he never made it. This bridge crossing was abandoned, and the new Lindley Bridge was erected downstream.

## HADLEY CREEK

Henrietta will have to muster all of her surplus energy to ascend the next group of swift rapids. On the west bank along this stretch of the river there are two tiny rivulets cascading down the steep slope of a very famous mountain. The second of these tiny streams is Hadley Creek. Lee Hadley told me that A. A. Hadley had an accident crossing this gulch. His horse threw him, causing his demise. Not many folks (including myself) knew this stream even had a name. I will tell you more about Mr. Hadley later along in the book.

Between Clear Creek and Hadley Creek, Henrietta's ancestors would have encountered an unusual scene. In December, 1955, the Mattole River was swollen to its limits from too much rainfall when another severe storm dumped thirteen more inches into the watershed. From seven in the morning until three in the afternoon it poured down. Across the Mattole River from the mouth of Hadley Creek, on the east side of the river, Mr. Andrews was enjoying his evening cup of spirits. His neighbor knocked on his door and informed him the river was rising much faster than it usually did during most storms. Mr. Andrews just laughed and raised his glass and saluted. "Let 'er rain," he said, "I'll ride 'er down if it gets up here." He either passed out or slept too soundly. The next morning his body was found lodged in a tree downstream. His cabin was scattered along the river bank here and there with the beating it had taken from the flood. Henrietta's ancestors, observing this chap struggling along in the muddy torrent, no doubt would have shaken their heads at the antics of humans. It was plainly no place for man or beast to have been, only fish.

## ROBERTS' HOLE

Soon Henrietta will arrive at the quiet waters of a deep pool. This is known as Roberts' Hole. The land surrounding this pool was in the Roberts family for years, and though it has changed hands, it still bears the Roberts name. Our proverbial fish, attempting to take a siesta on the bottom of this great hole, might have to dodge hundreds of lures.  Two types of people have found this pool attractive: fishermen and swimmers.  Once again, two more bodies may have been spotted and been shied away from by Hen's relatives.

Helen Adams, the sister of Louis Adams, was enjoying a swim in this deep pool.  She went under for too long, and it became obvious to Charlie Gilbert that she was in trouble.  He dove in to rescue her, and they both drowned, thus adding more stones to the Petrolia Pioneer Cemetery. Helen Adams was the descendant of a very controversial man in our history.  It was during the Civil War, and his name was John Brown.  We've all read about John Brown's role at Harper's Ferry.

## CONKLIN CREEK

Conklin Creek is the next tributary upstream to enter into the river.  Moses J. Conklin, the first postmaster of Petrolia, lived across the field from the pool just mentioned.  Before Moses owned this property, the Mattole Indians had an encampment here.  Mrs. Conklin, the former Margaret Chambers, is reported to be the first white woman on Mattole soil.  M. J. Conklin was involved in many facets of life.  I found it very interesting to learn that he grew a nice crop of tobacco one year.  I wonder why no one grows tobacco here today; or do they?

This creek has two main branches.  The ground between these two feeders has a name with which I can find no argument.  It is known as Middle Ridge.  Being in the middle of the two tributaries, it was a very likely title.  If all names were that uncomplicated, I could have finished this book years ago.

Where the Conklin merges with the Mattole, there once existed a grassy field known to lovers of picnicking as Runyon Flat. I have eaten a few sandwiches (and ants) there myself in the past. The homesite of the Runyon family (which I know very little about) is believed to have been across the little road on a narrow bench. Nothing else could I find about these people.

## MCGINNIS CREEK

This is the next creek in line which Henrietta will observe. The mouth of this creek also approaches the Mattole from the east, as does Conklin. The 1860 census tells me John McGinnis, age twenty-seven, an Irish lad, resided here. I have nothing else to report on this gentleman, but being of Irish descent, I am sure he must have done something wonderful in his stay along the Mattole.

## WIRE FENCE, HOMESTEAD, AND COW PASTURE OPENINGS

Before we continue upstream, let's take a side trip into the hills around these last two mentioned tributaries. Calvin "Hap" Stewart had lived on Conklin Creek over three quarters of a century. He related a few names to me (which some maps may or may not register) in this neck of the woods. Hap's ranch was owned in the early days by Charles Johnston. This gentleman was, no doubt, a very practical farmer. During his stay in these hills, wire fencing was introduced to the West, and he used the new material to fence in a grassy part of his ranch. Thus we have an unusual name: Wire Fence Opening.

Homestead Opening evolved from the settling of Hap's grandfather. I feel obligated at this point to explain what an "opening" is. It is a grassy meadow surrounded by forested land, and was often very attractive to early settlers. Believe it or not, there was once a dairy up in these hills. So, we have another name now, and it is Cow Pasture Opening. If you feel that all of this "opening" lingo is for the birds, you're right. Our next subject is Goose Bend.

## GOOSE BEND HOLE

Shortly after leaving the vicinity of these two creeks, our Henrietta is looking for a nice, quiet place to rest once again. A large deep pool called Goose Bend Hole will serve her purpose. Once upon a time one of Hen's ancestors could have been horrendously frightened by an event which I will now relate.

The river along a rocky bend in the Mattole at this location became the bedroom for thousands of migrating wild geese in the good ol' days. You and I will never witness such a scene as I am about to mention. When the honkers came south for the winter, they picked out certain locations to bed down for the night, and this stretch of the Mattole was one of their regular layovers. Any bird intelligent enough to fly south for the winter was also crafty enough to pick out a spot a long distance from the presence of a two-legged monster who carried the roaring fire stick which could rain birdshot down upon a goose's feathers. No goose had any desire to become a dinner on a settler's table, or to have its feathers stuffed into a pioneer's pillow. The cautious birds would come sailing into their nightly roosting place just at dusk when shooting was nigh impossible. The pioneers, having acquired a taste for goose, were not to be outsmarted by a silly old bird. One evening, several great hunters slipped into hiding spots at Goose Bend Hole before dark. Each man laid out his shotgun before him, and a pile of shells. The game was simple. After the geese landed, one man would rise up with a strong spotlight, and the other men would open fire at the resting birds. The fellow responsible for illuminating the darkness of night was a very methodical man, and in an attempt to prove to his fellow hunters he was reliable, he decided to check out the light. Cupping the light in his hand, he flipped the switch for one instant. You guessed it! If Hen was dozing in the bottom of that hole this night, she would have been scared out of her scales by the beating of thousands of wings on the water. All guns emptied into the place where there had been many goose dinners a few seconds before. I remember my mother telling this story, plus two more additional facts. My dad ate dried apples for dinner that night, not goose, and he was never asked to hold a light again for any future hunting expeditions.

## RAINBOW RIDGE

If the geese had flown eastward, in their frightened condition, they shortly would have passed over Rainbow Ridge. Early settlers referred to this chunk of terra firma — the land between this ridge and the valley — as the back country. In this vast area, there once roamed, literally, thousands of wild swine.

After the stock market crash, and the following Depression, there were many folks raising hogs in the Mattole. There were many pigs and no market for them; consequently, most ranchers just turned them loose to forage for themselves in the back country. This bacon on the hoof rooted its way further and further until reaching acorn country. The Indians were no longer present to use the acorns for flour, so the hogs flourished and grew into herds of what some people today refer to as wild pigs. The rooters were not alone in the hills. I could write an entire book on the strange happenings out in this locality, but I will contain myself to these few.

## BUCKEYE MOUNTAIN
One lump of soil is known as Buckeye Mountain. This name is derived from the buckeye trees growing there. When I was a wee lad, there was a lady living on this land. She dwelt there all alone, and actually seemed to enjoy the fact that there were no neighbors for miles around. She spent most of her leisure time wandering the hills collecting arrowheads which were left behind by the now departed Indian tribe. Many people who frequented the trail near her knew her actual name. Her real name was Bernice Cundiff. Most of us only called her Bonnie Buckeye. She had many cabins to live in, some of which were located on Prosper Ridge and Buckeye Ridge. When she wanted to eat seafood, she traveled to Prosper; if you happened to stop by her place on Buckeye, you might be offered coon for dinner.

To Bonnie's consternation, she was soon joined in these remote hills by a man named Lloyd H.

## ORIGIN OF MATTOLE

Brubaker. In 1916 the list of registered voters included him as a blacksmith. This gentleman, however, shared the same feelings as Bonnie. He also wished to live in seclusion. They both honored each other's feelings by never visiting until they finally entered hermit heaven. Today his claim is still called The Brubaker. His cabin had a most unusual design. One corner of the structure was built over a small rivulet. The little stream served as water supply, kitchen scrap disposal, and toilet. With his background as a blacksmith, I always expected that some day he would upgrade his facilities.

### BURGESS RIDGE
Between The Brubaker and the Mattole River, you will see on most maps Burgess Ridge. This title came to us in the form of A. A. Burgess. The Burgess family lived on the valley end of the ridge near the mouth of McGinnis Creek.

### VAN SCHOIACK
Another hummock of soil in the backcountry is named Van Schoiack. This homesteader's mysterious death became a great source of conversation for many years. It was said that he was murdered for some gold pieces which he had acquired shortly before his demise. The gold was never found, and some believe it remains hidden.

But, the story does not end there. If you were Mr. X, living in Petrolia, and you had a feud going with Mr. Z of the Honeydew area, it became the game of the times to blame your enemy for the murder. On the other end of the valley, Mr. Z was blaming it on

Mr. X. One oldster told me, after listening to all these tales, he was convinced that everyone in the Mattole had committed the foul deed. If you happened to be toting some twenty-dollar gold pieces in your jeans, your neighbor eyed you very distrustingly. What a lesson in psychology!

## THE PEG LEG

Just a little west of Van Schoiack is an opening with a few apple trees where I picked and ate the best apple I have ever tasted. This spot is known as The Peg Leg; a strange name to be sure, and it's lucky I am a curious soul or we may not know from whence this title came. When asking my mother about this property, I was told that she had once met a one-legged man on this land known as Peg Leg Sholtz.

## GROOMS RIDGE/EVERTS RIDGE

Moving slightly to the west along the backbone of this ridge I ran across two more names. Originally, this ridge was known as Grooms for the gent wearing that name. Later a Canadian by the name of John Everts settled at the same location and lo and behold, instead of the property wearing the title of Grooms, it was usurped by John Everts, and is now known on the maps as Everts Ridge. History forgot you, Grooms, but I didn't. I've at least given you honorable mention.

## SHERMAN'S PRAIRIE

In 1870, a man named W.H. Sherman was riding across this ridge when he fell from his horse. Sherman expired on the spot. He (so the story is told) liked to imbibe, and he was found frozen to death. If you ever find yourself in the vicinity of an opening called Sherman's Prairie, remember, there is a moral to the story about this landmark. Don't drink and ride; especially when it's freezing cold and snowing! There is more history to be told concerning this hill, but Henrietta is waiting for our return to Goose Bend.

## SHENANIGAN RIDGE

As Hen wiggles up over the riffle at the top of the deep hole, she might chance to observe a long ridge to her right. This we call Shenanigan. Three stories evolved, as I encountered this landmark, and I have chosen two of the best and most accurate. First, there is a true episode concerning two farmers from Union Mattole. They were on horseback, attempting to drive a herd of hogs to Petrolia. On the brow of the hill, where the dump site is today, one of the porkers strayed from the others. A stock dog was dispatched to round up that wandering slab of bacon. For some unknown reason, the dog got his signals mixed and went charging through the middle of the pigs causing them to scatter everywhere. May I stop right here and ask you a question? How would you react to this same situation? I, myself, would have turned the air blue with cute names for the dog. The dog's owner, however, was perhaps the first gentleman farmer. He merely crossed his hands on the saddle horn, looked all around and softly spoke to his companion. "Now, wasn't that a hell of a shenanigan?"

Further research informed me that this ridge bore the name long before the piggy incident. Back when the wars between the original inhabitants and the newly settled Caucasians were making history, a man lost his life on this ridge. John McNutt was riding horseback one day when he was bushwhacked by Indians along the trail leading to Cookie Mountain. McNutt, and a few other cowboys, were riding to help with a roundup. They were ambushed, and McNutt was fatally shot. The survivors of the attack returned to Petrolia where they were asked what had happened. They simply answered, "The Indians pulled a shenanigan on us." Lloyd Roberts, a long-time resident of the Mattole, related this information to me. His uncle was among those cowboys who were attacked. Thus occurred the true naming of Shenanigan Ridge. The tragedy of McNutt's demise took place in 1863, long before the scattering of the piggies. A few miles northwest of Petrolia, the first large creek the highway crosses bears Mr. McNutt's name yet today.

## THE DUTCHMAN

For over a decade I traveled the road which took me over Shenanigan each and every school day. As you break over the summit and descend northward toward Petrolia there are several nasty switchbacks. On one of these hairpin turns, the vehicle I was riding in did not negotiate the bend. This book, and also the author, were nearly a dead issue. Every writer is entitled to one gripe per manuscript. Here is mine. We have capabilities of putting a man on the moon, and raising taxes even higher than the moon, but still we are forced to travel this road which is not too much better than the trail McNutt was riding the day the Indians sent him to "the big roundup in the sky."

Amongst these switchbacks there was a grassy opening known to all as The Dutchman. In researching for this book, I finally learned why it was so called. Dutch Mike Shallard had a cabin here at one time. We'll hear more about Mr. Shallard when Henrietta gets closer to Honeydew.

## JIM CREEK

Once again, I traveled daily across this landmark in complete ignorance of its origin. Descending Shenanigan Ridge to the south, there is a small culverted creek. This is Jim Creek. Speaking with an old-timer who lived around this area as a child, I learned there was a mill at the mouth of this creek. It was a small mill operated by James Newton Dudley. The operation was of short duration and did not last long enough for the stream to gain the name of Mill Creek as did others along the Mattole, like at East Mill Creek. What he left behind here at this creek however, were some old mill remnants, and his first name.

## INDIAN CREEK

As we drop down the slopes of this mountain and join the flat land we cross over Indian Creek. Many of Henrietta's cousins have spawned up this stream. On the south bank, not far up the creek, there once was a large Indian encampment. The camp was uninhabited during the mid 1800's after white contact, but on July 23, 1919, President Woodrow Wilson granted 160 acres in the headwaters of this creek to Mary Ann Thompson, a Round Valley Indian.

# 9

# NEW JERUSALEM

### ELWYN LINDLEY BRIDGE

Henrietta passed Indian Creek and continued on around the next bend of the river. A large shadow on the water may cause her some momentary alarm; however, it is merely the Elwyn Lindley bridge. This looming structure was dedicated to Mr. Lindley for his many years of service to the county. He followed his father's career as county supervisor.

Standing on the Lindley bridge and looking upstream, one can see remnants of an old bridge which was replaced by this newer cement structure. The old bridge, built around 1920, was of iron components and planking. It was suspended by huge cables. That cable bridge spanned the river at the exact location of the old wagon crossing known as The Shields' Ford. I mention this because the Shields family lived nearby. Thomas Rochford Shields was seventy-five in 1906, according to census records of the time. They had a large family with nine children. When names were chosen for their children they seemed to have been ahead of their time. Today, we would think nothing of naming a child "Free Love Shields."

Mr. Shields enriched his property with many cherry trees. Unfortunately for him, neighborhood kids loved cherries; and when he was away, the kids would play—up in the cherry trees. One day, Mr. Shields slipped back unexpectedly, and surprised the cherry fanciers. He screamed like a banshee, and fired off an old blunderbuss loaded with black powder and balls. I interviewed Mr. "G" in his ninetieth year of enjoying cherries. He said, "Mr. Shields didn't see me fly out of that cherry tree due to the billowing gunsmoke, or he would have witnessed a new record set for the long jump." When the smoke cleared from that old muzzle loader, there were no cherry pickers left. None ever returned again!

## MILL CREEK (ANOTHER ONE)/ DANNYVILLE/WILD TURKEY CREEK

Slightly upstream beyond the spot where the old suspension bridge once hung, is our third, but not last, Mill Creek. For a relatively small creek, this stream roars into the river during the rainy season. It enters the Mattole from the west and starts low on the northeast side of Cooskie Mountain, which separates the valley from the ocean.

In the early days, the Millard Fillmore Gardner family operated a box mill here. Boxes were needed to package the fruit from numerous orchards in the valley. They used water from the creek to operate the sawmill. When the hard rainstorms of the winter filled the creek, the mill ran at full power. The only fault with this situation was that the Gardners lived on the opposite side of the river and would have to cross over the swollen channel to get to work. Many people living along the river in the early days had rowboats, and thought nothing of rowing across the flooded river any time they chose to do so. The Gardners were good boatmen.

Henrietta bypassed this creek because she had been cautioned about the gentleman who stood on the banks of this creek in the winter and jabbed at the unsuspecting salmon with his spear pole. Many of Henrietta's ancestors who didn't heed the warnings of their elders, climbed the creek to spawn.

Each winter I remember this fellow passing our home, and he would have his long pole with large hooks fastened to it over his shoulder. Sometime later I would see him returning from this Mill Creek with a big salmon in one hand, and his spear pole in the other. It was his favorite haunt, and he always seemed to be successful whenever he did his gigging. The most important thing that I remember about this chap was his lack of bathing. Yes, it was rumored that he never took a bath. With the combination of a little pitch from his kindling, a smattering of lamp black, and a generous portion of bacon grease, this man's facial appearance lost any resemblance to a white *Homo sapiens*. One winter day he walked by and spoke with me. I did notice that he had a rather peculiar, musty odor. I kept an eye out for his return that day. As dusk arrived, I thought I saw him trudging up the road, but the man who approached me had no hat, no spear pole, no fish, and a very white face. Confused, I ran up to the stranger and blurted out, "Excuse me, I thought you were Mr. `X.'" He said, "I am Mr. `X.'" It seems he had been standing on a mossy rock which was wet and slippery. When he jabbed his long pole at a big fish, he lost his footing and fell in. He tumbled over and over for a long way downstream. When he eventually crawled from the water, lo and behold, he was a white man again.

The flat where the box mill stood once was called Dannyville. Danny Spear dwelt here for a short time. Today, in 1996, if you were to ask a resident within ten miles of this location just where Dannyville was, all you would get is a blank stare. There are less than a handful of people existing today who ever knew that the Danny Spear family once resided in this area. Fortunately, I am one of them, for what good it does you.

Due to a prolific show of turkey feathers along this stream, and even many sightings of the wild birds that dropped them, the stream has recently been renamed Wild Turkey Creek. Personally I think that's fowl play.

## GARDNER CREEK/GREEN FIR MILL CREEK/ DRINKING WATER CREEK

The next major stream above Wild Turkey Creek was once known as Gardner Creek. Grover Gardner, whose father ran the box mill, had a claim at the headwaters of this stream.

In the middle of the Mattole timber boom, a

sawmill was built on a flat near the mouth of this creek. The entrepreneurs envisioned a true timber town complete with numerous crew cabins, a mess hall, and a large two-story sawmill accompanied by a stream-fed mill pond. These all became realities. Water for the mill pond was diverted from the creek, and soon it was being called Green Fir Creek. Ironically though, the mill never operated to saw even a single board. Whether by disagreement among the partners, or some nefarious scheme, its failure terminated the tiny town.

Shortly thereafter, the property was subdivided and all of the owners piped their domestic water from the creek. The newest title of the stream is Drinking Water Creek.

## COOSKIE MOUNTAIN

The water from these last two streams comes from Cooskie Mountain, that at 2,950 feet elevation, ranges high over the Mattole River which is said to be named for its "clear water." I had always heard that the name Cooskie was derived from the Coosic Indians that inhabited the vicinity (and I'm not sure I have the spelling of the tribe correct). While researching possible origins for the name of this mountain, I came across some interesting words that made me stop and take notice. In the Nez Perce Indian language, the word for "clear water" is koos-kooskia. Within twenty miles of Nezperce, Idaho, there is a little settlement called Kooskia, located fifty miles south of Clear Water River. There is a town named Cusick in the northwest corner of Washington. Is it possible that as migrations took place ages ago, indigenous people brought along a few words such as koos-kooskia?

## LOG CABIN HOLE

These two streams do not hold much enchantment for our Henrietta. Soon she finds herself resting comfortably in one of the deepest pools of the river. This pool once measured over thirty feet deep. Then the floods of 1955 and 1964 brought down gravel in sufficient amounts to fill in the hole belly deep on a short horse. However, much of the aggradation has migrated on downstream in the last three decades, leaving the pool deep once again.

There is a tiny creek running into this pool. Mapmakers did not think it was important enough to name it, so I did. Their theory must be, "If you can spit across it, don't name it." I have spent many happy hours of my life swimming and fishing at the confluence of this rivulet and the Mattole River. It only seems fair then in proclaiming this rivulet as Buck's Creek (your author's nickname). Near the turn of the century a log cabin stood here, but has since been claimed by antiquity. The cabin presently sitting on this site today is my humble abode, and within its walls is the desk and typewriter from which this conglomeration of memories was spawned. Henrietta, however, is only resting here. Her spawning will come later.

## ANNIE'S CABIN

Let's detour now up Buck's Creek as there is much history up there. I must take you back to the west end of Everts Ridge. On this west slope is an opening my family calls Annie's Cabin. My Aunt Annie homesteaded this land, and built a small cabin there. This homestead is where Buck's Creek originates. The old cabin wasted away long ago, but the name remains.

## GRAVEYARD HILL

Midway along Buck's Creek is a landmark we call Graveyard Hill. It has an actual graveyard at its summit. T.J. Dudley and Mr. Lambert rest here, among others. Lambert was killed on Cooskie Mountain in 1883, shot in the back under mysterious circumstances. All during my childhood I didn't understand the reasoning for selecting gravesites atop steep hills. All of the materials, including the deceased, had to be sledded up the steep hillside to the burial grounds. In doing research for this book, I found that the Dudleys preceded my family on this property before my ancestors purchased it.

If I seem vague on the subject of this cemetery, I have a good reason. Normally, I am not apprehensive of most graveyards, but I am always very nervous when I am near this particular one. When I was five or six years of age, my cousin and I took our toy shovels to this site and had us a digging good time. When our respective mamas learned of our expedition, we were severely tanned. You know where! I have an excellent memory, and the area around my back pockets still vibrates when I approach those tombstones.

There are many buildings that date back to the pioneer days. The Miner ranch house, where I was reared, is one of these. This landmark goes back to

1868, when my ancestors and the other Marysville settlers came by wagon into the Mattole. The house began with only a few rooms, but during its 120-year history many more were added totaling seventeen at present. Mattole got electric power lines in 1947, but long before that there was hydro power for this ranch house.

A spring bubbles from the ground atop a bedrock bench above the homestead. This little creek, with its waterfall, is largely responsible for the building being located where it is. My dad and uncle built a cement dam to collect flow from this spring, and from this point, water was piped down to house level where it ran a pelton wheel to generate electricity. A strong wire was secured to a spring-loaded shutoff valve, and it ran through pulleys over the wagon road to my parent's bedroom. When darkness came each evening, a large metal ring tied to the end of the wire was pulled down and fastened to a hook on the wall. This movement raised the lever on the shutoff valve allowing the force of the water to spin the waterwheel and the lights would come on. Later when everyone was in bed, the ring would be released from the hook, and the lights would go out. The excess water from the dam flowed down the creek and over the waterfall into a grotto that supports trillium and five-fingered fern yet today.

My mother lived a very healthy life here. She passed on at ninety-seven. She swept floors, fed her family, and hung out the wash for seventy years. Back in the hungry days of the Great Depression, many tramps learned that my mother was a great cook. Her early training would not let any hungry soul pass by her door without being well satisfied with her country cooking.  One of these frequent visitors was a bindle stiff (a hobo) who abused his privileges.  One day when my mother was in the back yard, this particular hobo entered her kitchen and simply helped himself to a big pot which was bubbling away on the wood range.  When confronted by her sudden return to the kitchen, the intruder blurted out, "Your stew isn't up to its usual this time, Mrs."  She laughed and told him that it was no wonder, as it was her spring cleaning rags which were being boiled after the morning cleaning.  Now that I give it some thought, I can't say that I remember this out-of-luck gent ever stopping at our ranch thereafter!

Mother Nature has given our egg-bearing fish a gentle nudge which reminds her that her time to create new fish life in the Mattole is near at hand and she should move along upstream.  Therefore, she moves her powerful tail with a few agitating strokes and propels her scaly form up the swift current.

## MATTOLE GRANGE HALL

A quarter of a mile upstream, Hen's keen senses may pick up a strange vibration being emitted at night from the dance floor of a very large building located on the river's east bank.  This is the site of the Mattole Grange Hall.  In 1874, the Grange was formed in downtown Petrolia at the corner of Sherman and Henderson streets, but its existence was soon terminated.  In the early nineteen thirties it was reorganized at the Harvest Festival grounds.  Before the reformation of the Grange, a giant celebra-

## ORIGIN OF MATTOLE

tion would be held each year, including horse racing, dancing, and a large produce display of the local harvest. This community project was known simply as the Harvest Festival. It took place on the grounds that we know today as A.W. Way County Park, very

*The Mattole Grange Hall has provided grounds for many celebrations through the years.*

close to the present Grange site.

As a wee lad, I saw my first magician pull a rabbit from his hat, ate at my first deep pit barbecue, saw my first horse race, and took my first airplane flight from this property. A dance hall, constructed from logs, was located across the road from the campground. It burned down one night shortly after its construction. After the fire, a new Grange Hall was built at its present location in Union Mattole. Since 1934, dances have been held at this new location. When several hundred pairs of boots begin stomping in unison to the beat of a red hot boogie, it makes lots of vibrations in all directions.

## NEW JERUSALEM

Another small building once occupied this property in very early days. It was a church. Rain or shine, folks would come over hill and dale from miles around to sing and pray here. On hot sunny days, the windows and doors would be left open, and the congregation could be heard singing from a considerable distance. If a stranger passing by should ask a resident, not in attendance, what the singing was about, he would be told that it was New Jerusalem.

One of the favorite routes taken by the worshipers was a trail up a mountain we previously mentioned. It went around Graveyard Hill and up past Annie's Cabin and on toward Everts Ridge. This was known as the Jerusalem Trail. Along this route were many of God's creations such as stately firs, giant oaks, monstrous pepperwoods, and thousands of bushes of poison oak. Did you ever wonder exactly where poison oak fit into the scheme of things? Me too!  I wouldn't have been upset if divine intervention (in answer to prayers from the parishioners traveling along the trail) reduced the quantity of those pesky plants.

In 1882, M.J. Conklin wrote in the newspaper about two grist mills located in the valley.  One was seven miles south of Petrolia on Squaw Creek in "New Jerusalem."  By 1930 this name had fallen from use, and the grist mill at Squaw Creek turned no more.  How times change.

## FALL CREEK

As Henrietta isn't fond of barbecue or dancing, we will follow her wake onward to Fall Creek.  High on the steep slope across the river from the Grange, there is a small drainage with no name I could find.  Mother Nature has created a picturesque waterfall high up near the source of this creek.  Since childhood, I can remember looking out our kitchen window at this roaring cascade of tumbling water after a heavy rainstorm.  I could get a good estimation of the previous night's rainfall by observing the boiling cataract.  This stream enters the river across from A.W. Way Park at the bottom of a very swift set of rapids.  All fish seem to sense what's ahead and take a siesta at this location.

A fisher friend and I were tossing spinners into this water one day, when I hooked and landed a nice steelhead.  Looking up the river bar, my companion noticed another fisherman approaching us.  Not wanting anyone to know that the fish were biting, I quickly slid the fish into the back of my old fishing jacket.  The lining was torn along one side, letting the slimy steelie slide in easily. I turned my back from the newcomer and stood there smiling like a kid who had just stolen candy but hadn't as yet been caught. When asked the usual question about our luck, our answer naturally was in the negative. Just then my fish made me out the liar I was attempting to become. One last flip of his tail broke more threads loose and he came flying out of the coat to land at my feet. There was a full minute of long, cold silence. The stranger rolled his eyes to the heavens and smiled. "If I were to cast into this hole," he announced, "just maybe a fish would fall from the sky and land at my feet also." With this statement he began fishing.

As the newcomer landed a couple of fish, he asked me the name of this pool. "When I get home," he said, "I want to tell my brother about this fine fishing spot." I grinned and told him it was now known as Fall Creek, where fishies fall from the sky.

## A.W. WAY COUNTY PARK

The river now makes a sweeping curve around A. W. Way County Park. These several acres are named for Arthur Way. He was the son of an English seaman, Henry Way. Henry came to Humboldt County in 1868 from Bridgeport, England.

Early in this century this flat, now used as a public park, was the valley's top entertainment center. A celebration known as the Harvest Festival took place here on Labor Day each year. As previously mentioned, there were many different events to be enjoyed on this great holiday. Plane rides, all types of horse races, produce displays, dancing, magicians, and last but not least, the best barbecue in the West.

I remember quite well my first flight in the barnstormer's biplane. I rushed to my parents to tell them about my flight. They were not very interested in hearing of my adventures as they were busy signing their names to the charter member roster of the newly reorganized Mattole Grange to be located at the Harvest Festival grounds. Their early membership is significant for the fact that the Grange soon thereafter moved to a portion of our ranch, and remains in that same location today.

High on the mountain, just south of Fall Creek, is an old abandoned homestead with stately chestnut trees called the Weinsdorfer. This Bavarian family once lived here on this hill.

I have a word for you ladies who are reading this page. When next you have a heated discussion with your man, it would behoove you to think of this tale I am about to relate. This story was handed down to me by a neighbor of the Weinsdorfers'. It seems that Mr. and Mrs. Weinsdorfer had very short tempers. The neighbor said he would always know if they were home by the loud discussions he could overhear from far away. One day he paid them a visit to see if the chestnuts in their orchard were ripe yet. He arrived only to find that the Mrs. was missing. Mr. Weinstaffer, as the name is frequently pronounced, was chopping kindling for his evening fire. When asked about his wife, he replied that she had gone looking for the cows. After a long visit, the neighbor noticed it was beginning to get dark, and the lady of the house had not yet returned. "It's getting dark," said the neighbor, "how long has she been gone?"

*Mr. and Mrs. Weinsdorfer stand at their doorway.*

"Two or three days," came the reply! "Good heavens, shouldn't we go look for her? Maybe she needs help." "She didn't need help to get lost," retorted Mr. Weinsdorfer, and he returned to making kindling. The moral here is, if you gals go out chasing cows, make darn sure you have a man at home who cares if you ever return.

## 10

# SQUAW CREEK TO BULL CREEK

### SQUAW CREEK

As Henrietta encounters Squaw Creek she most likely will not enter, even though it is the fifth largest creek in the Mattole watershed, and is fed by dozens of tributaries. Perhaps an inherited instinct warns her that her ancestors may have been frightened away by the noisy gristmill which was located near the mouth. However, a few hearty fish had to meet the challenge because Squaw Creek has always been a fine stream for salmon and their offspring.

    This particular gristmill was owned and operated by Mr. Milton Dudley. People as far away as Ettersburg traveled to Mr. Dudley's mill for their flour.

    Squaw Creek had the reputation of becoming muddy when the sky merely clouded over and even looked like rain. The cause of this was due to a gigantic landslide on the backside of Cooskie Mountain. When I was a little tyke, I asked why this creek was always murky. I was informed that it was from the ghosts of the squaws who were washing their feet in the stream. I regret to say that the actual fact of how the squaws became ghosts is not all that humorous. The tribe lived peacefully on a flat a short distance up this creek. There were a few disagreeable white men here that would not attempt the slightest peaceful negotiations with any Indians. One particular Indian hater slipped into their camps and left poisoned corn for them to find and eat.

I have to stop here and introduce a word of caution for you readers. If you get into an argument with your nearest neighbor and come home some day to find a box of corn flakes on your door step, don't eat them.

Sometime later an infamous Indian hater gathered a group of men together, and raided the village site. They massacred nearly everyone including women and children. There is no doubt in my mind that the murder of these people is the origin for the name Squaw Creek.

## THE CONCRETE ARCH

A long, long stone's throw upstream from Squaw Creek, Henrietta notices another shadow cast upon the water. Around 1920, a concrete bridge was constructed at this location. Before the bridge, there was a road available to travelers which ran along the west bank of the Mattole River at the base of Cooskie Mountain and crossed Squaw Creek near the Dudley gristmill. Due to extremely unstable terrain, the road was abandoned and bridges were built. Before the construction of the concrete arch, my father ferried my siblings across the Mattole to a schoolhouse on the opposite bank.

In December, 1955, an epic flood washed down

*The Concrete Arch spans the Mattole River just upstream of Squaw Creek and A. W. Way County Park. During the 1955 flood, water topped over the bridge.*

logs from a timber mill upstream in Honeydew. Water poured over the top of the bridge. As the logs rushed down the river they smashed into the bridge and demolished the cement railings. Steel railings now replace the original cement ones. When Henrietta's relatives passed by here during this particular event, they would have had two choices. They could swim under the bridge in a conventional manner, or could have taken the opportunity to be the first salmon to swim *over* a bridge.

## THE MILL POND

Up, up, and away. Is it a frog? Is it an otter? No, it's super fish: Henrietta! A few minutes of hard swimming and Hen will leave the Concrete Arch behind, and soon be resting in a long deep pool known as the Mill Pond. I fished here myself for a quarter of a century not knowing the origin of the name. In a conversation one day with Sam Kelsey, then the oldest resident of the Mattole Valley, I learned the answer. Sam had a timber mill here, and used this long deep pool as a holding pond for his saw logs.

Sam was born in 1856 and lived to the envious age of 112. He was a fabulous source of historical information. He had seen it all, and done it all. One day when I asked him his age he said he was ninety-nine. I remarked that I hoped to see him reach a hundred. Sam smiled, patted me on the back and said, "I don't see why not, you look healthy enough to me."

Sam Kelsey was a legend in his time. He worked at many jobs. He hauled freight into Petrolia, owned a sawmill, built coffins, did some doctoring, and even pulled teeth. If you could name a job, Sam had worked at it. Not far removed from the south bank of the Mill Pond is a large hump of ground anciently known as Kelsey's Knob. Because of Sam's activity in this area, I feel obligated to mention this landmark because very few people are aware of that title today.

## MARY'S FLAT

On the north bank of the Mill Pond there is a level piece of land called Mary's Flat. This property was owned by Mary Dudley. Milton Rice Dudley, who owned the gristmill at Squaw Creek, had a wife named Mary Amanda Dudley. William Green Dudley, Jr., Milton's brother, married a Mary too; Mary Smith from Ohio. Is it any wonder it was called Mary's Flat? Henrietta flips her tail at the question of which Mary was responsible for the name, and moves a short distance to a resting place at the bottom of the Mill Pond.

I was camping out here during deer season one summer when I was subjected to the most embarrassing moment of my life. It was nearly dark and I had just finished undressing right down to my bare hide. With blankets folded back, and prepared for sleep, I heard a loud crashing in the brush above my campsite. I jumped up and grabbed my rifle, worked the lever to inject a shell, and stood at attention ready to fire at whatever animal was coming my way. Was it a bear, cougar, or just maybe an enormous buck deer? WRONG! It was the neighbor girl taking a shortcut home across Mary's Flat.

## HADLEY HOLE

After that short rest, Henrietta moves on to next pool. This is called Hadley Hole. The origin of this hole's name was derived from a tragedy further upstream. From there, it wasn't logs that were floating into this pool, but the body of a Hadley girl. We'll hear more of this story as we reach the spot where the accident took place.

## BILL DUDLEY FLAT

Further upstream on the northeast side of the river is the Bill Dudley Flat. This was the same William Green Dudley, Jr., just mentioned back at Mary's Flat. Mr. Dudley had a sheltered location here for his large orchard. He was never rewarded with the fruits of his labor because he returned to his former home in Iowa. In 1899, he once again crossed the nation back to Humboldt County. I made the same journey in my camper around 1975. To me, this was a long hard trip. If I had to put on the same mileage with a horse-drawn covered wagon, you can bet your boots I wouldn't do it twice!

## TOM REED FLAT

Between the Dudley homestead and the top of Everts Ridge, a man called Tom Reed favored a certain spot that he purchased from Bill Dudley in 1879. This level bench, composed of 160 acres in the northwest quarter of Section 20, Township Two South, Range One West, cost Tom $550 in gold coin.

On the Fourth of July, 1899, a quilt was raffled off in Petrolia. The funds raised from this sale were donated for use at the Independence Day celebration.

Over one hundred names of prominent people were stitched onto this quilt. One of these was an oil driller named Tommy Reed. Of course, it is not conclusive that this Tom Reed lived at this location. However, with so few residents in the valley at this point in time, the chances of there being two Tom Reeds hereabouts are as good as me winning the lottery.

## THORNTON GULCH AND MAIL RIDGE

An unfortunate incident that occurred in the hills of the Mattole Valley was the murder of Mr. Thornton. He was on his way to town via Mail Ridge, the main travel route between the Petrolia and Upper Mattole post offices. As he crossed a creek between Mail and Everts Ridge, he was attacked and killed by Indians. He was a peaceful old man and carried no weapons. As a pacifist, he attempted to make peace between red and white factions, but his endeavors accomplished little and only resulted in his eventual death. Although he lost his life, he left his name behind as a legacy.

## HAZEL NUT OPENING

Before leaving this locality, I just have to tell you of another long-forgotten landmark. Across the county road and high on the ridge south above Kelsey Knob was a thick stand of hazelwood. The wagon train of the Marysville settlers made their very last descent from a ridge through an opening in this stand, and finally reached their goal at the floor of the Mattole Valley.

A homesteader who lived near this location was

an interesting topic of local conversation. He had gained the reputation of being the laziest man in the Mattole. Neighbors observed him picking his corn from a rocking chair. After reading this story over, I am not positive this fellow was actually lazy. He may just have been very inventive. When my corn is ready to pick, I intend to get a rocking chair and find out if it was actually a lack of ambition he was exhibiting.

When speaking of ambition, I am reminded of a fowl story. It is about a little chicken who was wondering why all the other chickens were eating and he was not. His mother said, "One has to scratch before one can eat." Believe me folks, I've done a whole lot of scratching through the dust of history to write these pages.

## THE ROCK HOUSE

While we are on the west side of the river, please indulge me to lead you along a quarter mile past Kelsey Knob, to a large flat area between the river and the county road. In the late 1930's, a local resident named Fred Roscoe had an inspiration to build a beanery in this location. Fred was a fine mason, and given plenty of available material, decided to build his structure out of river rock. After many years of laying stone upon stone, he finally accomplished his goal. He never did open the beanery, but in the height of the logging boom in the nineteen fifties an entrepreneur saw the need for a tavern and leased the stone structure for this purpose. It wasn't long before workers in the logging community were saying, I'll meet you at the Rock House for a drink.

# ORIGIN OF MATTOLE

Most of you reading this book have never, and will never, see the actual building, because it was torn down in the sixties after being damaged by a severe earthquake, so I've included a picture of it for you.

*The Rock House served as a tavern during the mid 1950's.*

The Wild West was still with us during the years that the Rock House flourished. I remember the stories of the cowboys who used to ride their horses into a barroom to order drinks for horse and rider. At the Rock House, it was a Jeep that nudged open the swinging doors, and then barged in and pushed all the bar stools down to one end of the bar. The motor raced as the driver slipped the clutch and yelled at the top of his voice: two beers for a couple of steers!

## ROSCOE FORD
Upon leaving Hadley Hole, Hen needs to negotiate a long stretch of rough water for a mile or so before reaching the Roscoe Ford. Here she encounters a very shallow riffle used by the pioneers as a wagon crossing. It was not always shallow enough though, and two men drowned while attempting to ford the flooded crossing.

## PRITCHETT CREEK
Switching back over to the northeast side of the Mattole River, this creek held an attraction for James Pritchett and his family, who built a cabin along it in 1860, according to Will Roscoe's book entitled *A History of the Mattole Valley*. On the 1970 U.S.G.S. quad map for Buckeye Mountain I found this creek spelled Pritchard. Other maps refer to J. Prichard living here in 1865, but I am going to stick with the spelling of Pritchett. If I am mistaken, I am not the first to be so when trying to factually document history. While reading other histories of the region I uncovered a knee slapper. I came across a book that read: "Happy Camp is located ninety miles west of Crescent City." Any town west of Crescent City, California, would be slightly soggy!

Wesley Roscoe settled near here and became the first postmaster for Upper Mattole around 1881. Mr.

Roscoe came to the West from New York. He braved storms, Indians, snakes, and all the other terrible hardships that pioneers like him had to endure on the journey westward.

In 1961, Mattole logging crews were transporting logs on a large scale. One afternoon, a tourist driving a fancy car entered my front yard. I noticed it had New York plates. When the man emerged from behind the wheel, it was apparent that he was all shook up. "I've been dodging all those logging trucks," he said. "Can you direct me to a better road back to the freeway?" I told him that there were two other roads, but that they were both worse than the one he had been traveling. Consequently, he hired a rancher's son to drive him back to the safety of four lanes. I don't think New York is turning out any more hardy pioneers these days!

## GRANNY CREEK

Henrietta may have spent some time at the Roscoe Ford checking its gravelly bottom to determine suitability for spawning. She must not have liked the conditions because shortly thereafter she moved on and approached Granny Creek. It's possible that one of Hen's kinfolks could have chanced a rare meeting with a wagon containing a newly married couple. Believe it or not, as far back in time as we are speaking, honeymooners tied a string of tin cans to the rear of the wagon. Many of these weddings were performed by Ernest Roscoe at his home on Granny Creek. Another resident of Granny Creek was Mrs. Wilkenson. She was known to all as Granny Wilkenson. This is how we come by the title of

Granny Creek.

A few hundred feet upstream from Granny Creek was the site of an early oil well in the Upper Mattole area. Local men formed a mining company, with oil being their primary goal. The company contracted much land from Squaw Creek to Honeydew. I don't intend to write many lines concerning oil along the Mattole, but this particular well is unique. Oil was taken from this shallow well at less than seventy feet. This was in 1865, and yet today, ninety-nine percent of the oil under the Mattole Valley is still there.

## DAMON, HARRIS, AND MOODY RIDGES

Following a map up Granny Creek, we encounter many ridges. Most of these derive their titles from folks once living there. Damon Ridge was named for E. C. Damon. He didn't stay long but his name did. He left the valley in 1870.

I learned that in the 1860's, Alfred Harris had lived on what we now call Harris Ridge. Mr. Harris had an Indian wife. Her brother, Jack, was adopted by Mr. Harris. There will be more about Jack later.

There was a man who came west from Ohio to live in these hills and raise livestock. His name was Thomas Moody. The 1860 census verified that he lived at this location, and for a young man of only thirty years old, at that time he had a fortune. The census valued his personal estate at $6,000. When gathering historical facts for this particular ridge, I was asked if this was the man's real name or his disposition. I replied, "The census only tells us that he was here, not his state of mind."

## MOOREHEAD RIDGE

The following is a fine example showing how I obtained much of the information I have accumulated. A letter came to me from Gladys Barnwell of Chalk Mountain. She mentioned that her family once dwelt in the Mattole Valley. Her father, Philo Moorehead, had property here, and she still remembered their cabin which was near the head of Spanish Creek. Thanks to all the many letters such as Gladys', I have gleaned the necessary information that I set out to find.

I neglected to speak of the elk which once roamed Moorehead Ridge. The vast herds of elk, which thrived in the valley along the river, used a certain trail to make their way each year to the west where feed was, no doubt, better. This trail was so well traveled, it became rutted three or four feet deep from the pounding of the hooves.

A law was passed in 1873 making it a felony to shoot an elk. I have to interject a story right here. Recently, a man came to Humboldt County to do a little deer hunting, but it was not a little deer that he shot. It was a monster! It took two or three friends to load it into his pickup. He took it to the proper authorities to have his giant deer validated. WRONG! You guessed it, it was an elk. The 1873 law read: "Two years in the slammer." This was one of life's little embarrassing moments.

## TELEGRAPH RIDGE

This title misled me. First I jumped to the obvious conclusion that telegraph wires had been strung along this ridge. Later I acquired the actual origin of this land's name from a real old, old-timer. He said that the Indians had no newspaper or TV, but they did have a primitive means of getting a message to grandmother's hogan. On certain peaks they would build fires and send up smoke signals. Their messages were telegraphed from here to there without the aid of wires. Telegraph Ridge also served as a primary trail between the Mattole Valley, Squaw Creek, and the coast. On some maps, it is labeled Telegraph Peak.

## COOK GULCH

Like a flea on a hot stove, my writing takes you hopping from atop Telegraph Ridge, back down to Granny Creek to follow Henrietta's meandering on upstream to Cook Gulch.

The water in the Cook Gulch Creek pours down from Cook Ridge. Isaac Cook was the man who lived here. He was a brother of Charles Cook, a resident of Petrolia. Charles Cook came west in 1854 from New York. He operated a freight line from Ferndale to Petrolia. This was long before any roads were built into the Mattole, and he traveled the beach most of the way. I believe that he was the first one to haul an organ into the Mattole. This musical instrument was slung by rope between four mules. Mr. Cook, being a good teamster, no doubt, delivered that instrument in perfect condition. Recently I received a package delivered by one of our freight carriers, and it was so badly damaged that I believe it could have been dragged into the Mattole behind four mules and been no worse for wear. Quality doesn't always improve with age.

## SAUNDERS CREEK

Saunders was once a schoolteacher in Petrolia. He lived near the mouth of this stream in 1876. When I was very young I went to this location to observe some foxes. The Roscoe family had a silver fox farm here for many years. Most salmon shun Saunders Creek, but Henrietta may be attracted to a larger creek on the north side of the river not much further along.

## SINGLEY CREEK

This creek may not appear on some maps, but it exists nonetheless. It was near this little stream that a fort was constructed during the troubled time with the natives. Camp Olney was named for its commanding officer, and was built in 1860. Today, if you were to confront a resident of the Mattole Valley and inquire about the location of this historical landmark, the most likely response would be, "Huh?"

After the Indian wars were over, the fort was abandoned. At this time it was converted into a store and saloon. A man with a colorful name, Mr. Green Brown, became the first proprietor in 1865. The store had a short life, closing when he died in 1866. Tobacco and liquor were two of the main items he carried. In Mr. Brown's case, the local gossip claimed he was his own best customer.

The reason for the title of this drainage is because of the presence of Mr. George Singley. He, not alone, owned property in this area. The Singley name is prominent, and can be seen in many other locations in the county as well.

## HADLEY CREEK

After passing by the previous location and all of its colorful history, Hadley Creek is the next creek Hen bypasses, but not for the same reason her ancestors would have. Hen's aspirations are further upstream, but her ancestors may have been repelled by mechanical commotion. At one time a gristmill was in operation on this stream on the opposite side of the river from Coon Ridge. It was owned and operated by Mr. George Hill, and functioned as late as 1920. My reason for not introducing this stream as another Mill Creek is because I wish to pay tribute to Mattole's first pioneer, Alfred Augustus Hadley. He settled along this creek in 1853. Sometime during his ranching career, he introduced merino sheep to the Mattole Valley.

Mattole Valley became a new source of lamb chops for the dining tables of northern California. By 1950 there were approximately one hundred and fifty thousand woollies roaming the Humboldt County hills, plus a few coyotes. Today, there are very few woollies left, but there are countless numbers of well-fed coyotes. I refer you to the bumper sticker on the sheepman's pickup truck which reads:

> **Eat Lamb, 10,000 Coyotes Did**

In the fall of 1995, a friend of mine was given two white female sheep. Their new owner said that she always wanted to have a black lamb for a pet. The ram that was introduced to the two ewes was also white, so my friend said a silent prayer asking providence to rain and deliver her a black pet. When lambing season rolled around, one ewe had twins, and the other had triplets. All five of them were black. When I learned of her good fortune I asked if she would seek a miracle for me. "I want next week's lottery numbers," I told her.

Mr. Hadley led an exciting lifestyle. His favorite pastime was hunting big grizzly bear. He had a special weapon tooled for this explicit purpose. It was a sixty caliber muzzle loader! If the ball missed, the concussion would surely get the bear.

Staying along the north bank, our aquatic friend Henrietta will find another large shadow on the river cast by a bridge. This bridge was important to folks living on the east side of the river who would no longer have to risk drowning while crossing the Mattole at this locality. It was connected to a road which had been constructed along the northeast side of the river from Holman Creek to Honeydew, known as the Holman Grade, which due to massive landslides was later abandoned.

## COON RIDGE

Not far above Hadley Creek we delve into another historical tragedy. In the days before any bridges, if they wanted their mail, local residents had to row their boats across the river to collect it. The Hadley family lived on the west side of the Mattole. The post office was on the east side. The two Hadley girls attempted to cross the swollen river, lost control of the boat, and drowned. Jack Harris, from Harris Ridge, who happened to be nearby, dove into the river to grab the young ladies, but unfortunately lost his life too. I wish to say, this boating accident took place during the winter of 1904, and nearly a hundred years later we still refer to the first pool above the Mill Pond as the Hadley Hole. This is where one of the young ladies' bodies drifted to, and was eventually found.

East of the site of the boating accident, and south of Mail Ridge, most maps show Coon Ridge. My first thought was, someone must have killed a coon here, and made history. I was partly right. A settler named John Coon, according to the 1860 census, did live here. You can also be sure that Mr. Coon probably killed more than one coon while residing on this ridge.

Our friendly fish Henrietta is not concerned with raccoons or the type of mail just mentioned. Traveling upstream is her male route, and she heads that way to see if there is any male waiting for her.

## HOLMAN CREEK

Holman Creek runs off of Coon Ridge through property that once belonged to the Holman family. Now, the Lindley family, relatives of the Holmans, continue on at this location, and the Holmans have departed. Although most maps don't register a title for this creek, there are still folks who remember it as Holman Creek.

## KENDALL GULCH

At the end of the Hadley property, Hen might nose around for awhile in the water emitting from Kendall Gulch. As I come to this confluence, I am a little perplexed. There is no darn name as a creek, it's only called a gulch. Why? Just like the other gulches already encountered, it seems there isn't as much dignity conferred on it by calling it a gulch. Marion A. Kendall lived here at the mouth of the creek in 1921, according to the Belcher Abstract and Title Company map at the County Recorder's office. She was a schoolteacher, and I wish I could talk to her and find out why the ravine was named for her, and not the water moving through it.

## DIRTY CREEK

Have you heard the expression, "Here's mud in your eye?" Henrietta quite possibly will have mud in her eyes while passing this creek. You won't find the name Dirty Creek on most maps, but this brown water constantly oozing into the river earns its title. This stream drains a slide area which made the Holman Grade impossible to maintain.

## SPRING CREEK

Spring Creek is a hop, skip and a jump from Kendall Gulch. You also won't find this one named on most maps. It is hardly more than a trickle on a hot summer day, but it is mentionable only for the fact that it was the source of water for the first auto-court in the valley. On the southern perimeter of this resort, a cafe once served Mattole's tourists. The proprietors of this establishment were very faithful at checking their rain gauge to record the local rainfall. In 1958, the total rainfall was four yards, two feet, and six inches! Recently, this record was broken. I only mention Mattole's moisture content to remind the readers who don't live in this watershed that, friends, it still does rain here.

In studying old history books, I learned that one

of our Presidents did not admire our wet season in Humboldt County. Ulysses S. Grant was in charge of Fort Humboldt in 1853. His theory was that the cold and dampness of the area drove him to imbibe of spirits to warm his chilled body. If anyone were to observe your author smiling happily in the middle of a driving rainstorm, it is because I share the same malady of Mr. Grant and occasionally the very same cure.

## WOODS CREEK

The next creek on the southwest side is Woods Creek. This stream has a decent flow in the wintertime, and I have observed many, many of Henrietta's cousins resting in the pools. Somewhere along this creek there actually was a man residing here by the name of John Woods. The 1906 census recorded him as a laborer.

In a good ol' Mattole history book, it was reported that John Alfred Woods entered into a heated discussion with his neighbor one day. The neighbor lost his cool and threatened Woods. Much later, the neighbor returned toting a firearm. At the neighbor's appearance, John grabbed his gun and shot the visitor. Now, it seems to me that this type of behavior would eventually make for a drastic shortage of neighbors. Not only that, but if he continued with that sort of neighborly relationship, the next census would report his occupation as gunfighter.

## BUNNEL PRAIRIE CREEK

Here I must take you back to the massacre on Squaw Creek. One of the few survivors of this battle was a young Indian boy. Somehow he found his way to the home of Mr. Bunnel, who lived in the grassy opening of this name. Mr. Bunnel was a blacksmith by trade, and he put the lad to work in his shop. When the smithy left the area, he sold the youngster to another man for a twenty dollar gold piece. This good samaritan was the gentleman from Shenanigan Ridge: Mr. Shallard. He took the boy to Bear River where he was placed in the hands of a rancher. This rancher and his wife had several children, so one more chair at the table was of little consequence. He was given the family's name, and as he grew up, he became quite well-known in this locality. There are several people still among us who can remember this survivor: Squire Morrison.

## HUNTER BLUFF
Hardly any of Henrietta's relatives have been known to investigate Bunnel Creek. Hen passes it up too. A whoop and a holler upstream is a slumping area we call Hunter Bluff. This slippery, sliding mountain, which for decades has been falling into the roadway, was named for Judge Hunter, a well-known rancher. The Judge was a land baron. At this location there is a shallow spot in the Mattole River known as the Hunter Ford, which was another crossing once used by horse and wagon. One man lost his life while trying to cross when the river was too high.

## DIVORCE FLAT
Between Hunter Bluff and Honeydew is a sign along the county road which reads Divorce Flat. This sign does not come under the heading of ancient history,

but it is making history.  Several eligible bachelors once lived in this neighborhood.  Now, who says it does not pay to advertise?  This sign surely must have been responsible for wedding bells ringing for most of these fellows.  Today they are saying, "Yes, dear," when the request is made, "Honey, do this," or, "Honey, do that."

In 1955, a sawmill was located here at Divorce Flat.  It was from this location that the cold deck at the mill was washed downstream by the flood that occurred that year damaging the Concrete Arch.  I mention the cold deck, because fifty years from now there may be no timber operations of that scale.  Some readers decades from now may assume that I am speaking of a deck of cards, which had grown cold, in the hands of some gambler.  Most sawmills stockpiled logs to enable them to run all winter without doing actual logging in the rainy season.  This huge stack of timber was known as the cold deck.

## PARKHURST RIDGE

Jumping across the river from Divorce Flat, your map shows Parkhurst Ridge.  Yes, you guessed it.  There was a Mr. Parkhurst who lived there.  William Parkhurst was a Baptist minister who came to this area with the Marysville settlers.  Let's stop and review the route that the reverend would take each Sunday to church.  It was a two or three hour horseback ride over ridges and across canyons, down the Jerusalem Trail, to his little church.  Nowadays it is nigh impossible to convince some of the public to drive ten minutes for an appearance at any one of several churches.

## UPPER NORTHFORK

Let us now catch up with Henrietta. She swam on ahead while we dallied around with history back in the hills. Fish cannot read, of course, but if Henrietta could, she would be confused by the name of the creek where we find her. She's resting at the mouth of another northfork, and this has always had me confused too. How can there be two northforks? I wonder how many other streams there are in the world that have two northforks. Anyway, for what it's worth, this is Upper Northfork. As Henrietta rests her tail, our tale continues up the upper.

Several tributaries make up the headwaters of the Upper Northfork. They are Devil's Creek, Oil Creek, and Rattlesnake Creek. The combination of these tribs results in the Upper Northfork being one of the largest streams in the system.

The reason for the title of Devil's Creek comes from the extremely steep headwall terrain that the old-timers called Devil's Hole. Adjacent to this creek is Devil's Hole Prairie. Devil's Creek actually turns into Oil Creek.

Oil Creek is bounded between Long Ridge and Rainbow Ridge. I find it unbelievable that anyone would not grasp at once the reason for this stream's title. Yes, many people have observed the sheen of oil on the water. There are countless seeps of natural gas in this region too. They can be lit and burn for days. There is enough written in other books about oil wells, so I won't spend more time here talking about it.

In the vicinity of Oil Creek is a place called Gravelly Flat. I don't suppose it was too gravelly for a homesite, because Squire Morrison built a cabin here. You'll remember, he was the Indian boy who escaped from Squaw Creek and grew up on Bear River.

The name Rattlesnake Creek, to me, has an ominous origin. These reptiles flourish in this particular area, most likely because of the torrid climate. Unfortunately, many of these slithering, rattle-tailed poison packers get washed down the Upper Northfork during high water and find a new home in Honeydew and vicinity. Fortunately though, for me, none of them take up residence in the valley below Squaw Creek. My family has lived snakeless on this ranch since arriving in 1868.

The broad ridge between Oil Creek and Rattlesnake Creek is called Curless Prairie. Low on the ridge near the confluence of these two tributaries is a cabin at the end of a long winding road. Guy Curless spent a lot of time at that cabin. He lived most of his life roaming the hills and canyons of southern Humboldt, hunting and trapping. I feel fortunate to have enjoyed many visits with this gentleman, and always went away enriched by new stories of his adventures. The cabin site is not far from Moonshine Valley. Yes, at one time there were many happy varmints chewing the mash from numerous stills on Bull Creek Mountain.

When Stan Roscoe perused an early draft of this manuscript, he mentioned that I hadn't said a word about The Gushaw. He was, of course, correct. The meager notes I had on it were misplaced, but after finding them, and being encouraged to share them, here is what I can tell you. The first tributary of the Upper North Fork, flowing down from the south slopes of Parkhurst Ridge, is called Gushaw Creek. In 1895, George and Rachel Gushaw lived in the proximity. I remember my father, and his friends in the Roscoe, Lindley, and Etter clans, referring to "huntin' on the Gushaw." The term was in wide use earlier this century, but only a handful are still familiar with the location. Today the property is owned by the Etter family.

## RAINBOW RIDGE

The large mountain at the headwaters of the Upper Northfork, standing at 3,542 feet, is called South Rainbow Peak. The ridge that connects this mountain and Rainbow Peak, to the north, is called Rainbow Ridge. Rainbow Ranch is situated at the top of Curless Prairie along Rainbow Ridge.

I have three plausible tales concerning the origin of the name for Rainbow Ridge. First, I was told that the ridge takes the form of a rainbow from a long distance view. Secondly, and not confirmed, I heard that a huge rainbow was observed by the first group of surveyors while originally mapping the area. A man of pioneer status told me the third version. He said that he had once asked Squire Morrison about the Indian's first arrival to this land. Squire solemnly responded, "The Indian descended from the sky in a big basket. We came down from a large rainbow." I am sorry to admit that my research could do no better than this. Personally, I like the last choice. After all, I wasn't around at that time, and can't dispute it!

More folklore handed down about Rainbow involves a story of two adventurers on this mountain for the first time. They saw a rainbow touching the silver fir. I could find no instance of any silver fir growing here. Perhaps the elevation is not sufficient.

## GREEN RIDGE

Green Ridge is located west of Rainbow Ridge, and separates Devil's Creek from Oil Creek. I regret that the only information uncovered by my questions to old-timers who were familiar with this spot was that Green Ridge seemed to retain its color much longer into the summer than did adjoining ridges. However, I did find a cute yarn concerning a man who had once lived here.

In looking back at history, I find that times would be good for awhile, and then things would go bad and there would be tough sledding. During one of these rough rides, a man who resided near Green Ridge came to Petrolia seeking work. He took a job shepherding a flock of sheep near the mouth of the Mattole. After a few months he came back to his employer and casually asked, "Do you still want me to caretake sheep?" "I do," came the reply, "but why do you ask?" "Well," came the answer, "if you do then you will have to fetch me some more sheep 'cause the coyotes have eaten up them others."

# 11

# BULL CREEK TO HONEYDEW

## BULL CREEK MOUNTAIN

Henrietta does not move upstream very far before she encounters another long shadow on the water. This shadow is cast from the bridge that allows traffic to cross over the Mattole River at Honeydew and continue along the road over Bull Creek Mountain to the 101 freeway. Hold on, if you cannot find the words "Bull Creek Mountain" on any maps; I can only tell you that old-timers have always called it this. Actually, the road takes you up and over a mountain and down the other side to Bull Creek. I am positive Hen couldn't care less about the origin of Bull Creek, but I know you'll be interested.

Grace Baxter, a longtime resident of Bull Creek, gave me this story. Back when the first immigrants settled west of the Eel River, there were still Indians living in the territory. A rancher brought a herd of cows to the rainbow country, along with his prized bull. One day the bull was missing, and he followed its tracks to the creek bottom on the flat, where he found a big fire burning which was surrounded by happy Indians. The jovial attitude was a direct result of the immense barbecue that they had just consumed. When asked about the source of their feast, the rancher was told that it was a big bull that had wandered into their camp. "So many bull come here," the chief said, "all Indians call this place Bull Creek."

I led you down the east slope of this mountain for this story to be told. Now let's return to the top of Bull Creek Mountain.

## PANTHER GAP
One of the famous landmarks found while traveling the Bull Creek road westward is a side road near the summit marking the vicinity known as Panther Gap. Many stories reached my ears about Panther Gap. The following lines have been chosen as the most accurate.

A local trapper was hailed one day by a resident of Bull Creek Mountain. He had just seen the largest panther in existence. The trapper immediately drove to the spot where the cat had been sighted, and investigated the area. The huge cat was reported to have been standing with his front paws on one log, and his back paws on another. When the trapper measured the distance in between, it measured nineteen feet! This didn't even account for the length of the tail. This occurred at a location where the mountain dips down to form a gap in the ridge.

Another account I'll pass along is more sobering. A small boy disappeared in this location. Tracks from a large panther were found, but the boy never was.

When I was a small lad, I was riding on horseback with relatives in this area when a panther crossed the road in front of us. Many other panther sightings have been reported in this locality over the years. Choose which story you wish, but regardless, the panther gets the credit.

## CATHEY'S PEAK AND WINDY NIP

An airplane flying over Bull Creek Mountain would have to stay above 3,620 feet. This knob is Cathey's Peak. Again, I found help by consulting the 1860 census. John Cathey, a farmer from Missouri, owned land in this area. He came west, and liked the area so well that he sent for his brothers to join him. According to Louise Mathison of Alderpoint, John Cathey is buried on the mountain that is named for him.

Traveling west along on the county road, this peak is on the right. After passing Cathey's Peak, we come out onto an exposed ridge called Windy Nip. The wind whistles across this ridge from either north or south almost constantly.

## GREGG PEAK

Less than a mile southwest of Windy Nip, Gregg Peak protrudes into the air 2,425 feet. On a very wrinkled map that someone loaned me to study, I learned that the Gregg family lived in this vicinity. Unfortunately, there was a bad tear in the map and now I haven't the foggiest idea of his first name.

Likewise, I have no knowledge as to the extent of their habitation, but I don't think they stayed around for long. And, that would be understandable, because if it was a winter when Bull Creek was white with several feet of snow, they could have been very discouraged and sought a warmer climate. Personally, I think snow is better on Christmas cards.

## POWDER FLAT AND NIGGER HEAVEN

As we descend this hill toward Honeydew, two names may come to mind that I must mention. One is Powder Flat. Explosives had to be used in constructing this section of the Bull Creek road. The place where the crew stored the dynamite is still called Powder Flat nearly eighty years later.

About halfway down the grade was the road crew cook shack. I was told in an interview with the foreman of the crew that a black cook was hired. When his chores were all caught up, he would sit on the front porch of the cook shack in a rocking chair, and relax in the sunshine. Passersby, when exchanging salutations, would always get the same reply. He would broadly grin and say, "Oh man, this here is nigger heaven." Today, because of racial sensitivity, the name has been shortened to simply: The Heaven.

Before the construction of this roadway only a trail existed. In an interview with another old-timer, Gene Landergen of Honeydew, I was told a fowl story. It involved a turkey drive that he went on when he was just a lad. It was slow traveling, driving these birds up the mountain, and they had not made it even halfway to the cook shack by the evening feeding time. If turkeys could talk, a conversation could have gone like this: "Tom, hiking is fun, but enough is enough! I'm hungry and it's already past supper time, so let's go home." With this declaration, the entire flock turned around, flapped their wings, and sailed back down to the valley.

It's time for us to sail back down to the valley too. If we stop on the bridge over the Mattole at Honeydew, and gaze down into the river we just might see Henrietta snoozing. She has enjoyed a nice nap while we've been working.

# 12

# HONEYDEW TO ETTERSBURG

## HONEYDEW

The town of Honeydew had its beginning around 1920. Levi Thrapp, a man with an eye on the future, constructed a building which has served as store and post office ever since. With the exception of one small home across the street, the store is the entire town of Honeydew. Many strangers entering the Mattole Valley have passed right on by Honeydew without even knowing they had done so.

One incident that I remember revolves around two fellows in a big shiny Cadillac. They rolled down off of Bull Creek mountain with brakes smoking, clattered across the little metal bridge, turned right and headed off in the direction of Petrolia. Two miles on down the road they encountered a man on horseback. They screeched to a halt and asked to be directed to the town of Honeydew. The horseman

ORIGIN OF MATTOLE

pointed back the direction they had just come from, and said, "Two miles, can't miss it." The driver turned to his companion and said, "You can't believe these hill people, we'll find Honeydew up ahead here somewhere." With that, they roared away.

Speaking of believable people, here is a story concerning an experience I witnessed on the Honeydew Store front porch. On this porch, history has been observed, and sometimes altered a bit, by colorful characters passing time and enjoying conversation. Most every sunny day you can find the bench crowded with local residents, and visitors passing through town. One day while I was sitting on the porch, I overheard a traveler engaging a whiskered resident in conversation. The bearded one pointed at a high ridge to the left and stated that he lived way up there. The visitor mentioned that he would like to pay him a visit and see the view. "Well, if you plan a trip up in those hills, be sure it's before dark, or the duodenums will get you." "And what is a duodenum?" queried the gullible stranger. "Well sir, it's a small animal like a pig, sort of, with a long snout like an elephant. With the hollow snout, they suck up blue clay from mud holes, and when they see a human, they shoot mud balls at 'em. Why, just last week I was walking up there after dark, and they attacked me. I had a brand new jug of muscatel wine in my hand when they shot at me. They must have hit me in the head and knocked me out, 'cause my neighbor found me laying there the next morning with my empty jug."

At this juncture in the conversation, I left the two fellows still talking on the front porch of the Honeydew store and returned home to consult my dictionary. I learned that we are all closer to duodenums than we might realize.

Now we finally get to the origin of the name for the crossroad settlement of Honeydew. If a bird lands in a tree at the Honeydew store, its feet get sticky with a sappy secretion. This product is a combination of insect excrement and the essence of certain tree species. This messy moisture is known as honeydew.

If this same bird, now with sticky feet, were to fly off southwest over the brushy mountains, it would soar over a grassy opening shaped like a violin. This is Fiddle Prairie.

*The town of Honeydew is served by this building which provides a store, gas station, post office, and a front porch for telling tall tales.*

Near Fiddle Prairie, some maps show a spring that issues out at 2,600 feet elevation. The fact that this is a relatively high elevation for a spring, and that it is near North Slide Peak, may be why it is titled Pinnacle Spring. But it is labeled wrongly, and here is the real name and the true origin. It is called Pinochle Spring. A group of local ranchers, quite fond of deer hunting, camped in this location each hunting season. In the heat of the day hunting is very poor, as big bucks hole up in some hidden cool spot. The hunters rested at this place and enjoyed their favorite card game: Pinochle.

## HONEYDEW CREEK

It's time once again to rejoin our fictitious fish, who is still resting in the shadow of the Honeydew bridge. Not far upstream is Honeydew Creek, which is one of the larger tributaries in the Mattole basin. It still has extensive acreage of ancient forest, and so, is one of the healthiest creeks in the Mattole.

The harassment Henrietta has endured so far, by the numerous lures and worm-laden hooks tossed at her during her journey up to this point, is about over. Honeydew Creek is the upper legal boundary for fishing. Her adventures will be blessed with one less danger as she continues on. Even though Hen passes by Honeydew Creek, many of her relatives are drawn back up it, as it has always supported an excellent fishery.

The first tributary of Honeydew Creek is called Beartrap Creek. This stream drops down from Beartrap Ridge out of the west. In the early history of the Mattole, traps were set along this ridge to capture the abundant population of bear. These traps were made of small logs stout enough to contain the large creatures. One reason that could account for great numbers of bear congregating in this vicinity is the dense growth of huckleberry brush. The bear and I share a common taste. Huckleberry pie is my all-time favorite dish.

Even though there is no fishing allowed in Honeydew Creek now, there was in the early days, and Henrietta's ancestors had an obstacle to encounter as they passed the mouth of Honeydew Creek.

An Indian encampment once existed near this confluence with the main river. Because smoked salmon was an important provision for winter food, they lived near at hand to their meal ticket.

During the wars between the Indians and early settlers, a surprise march was conducted on this camp. Nearly all of the Indians were annihilated. The attack came while most of the tribe were in their sweat lodge. Whatever cure they anticipated from the steam was no remedy for the hail of musket balls which assailed them.

Let's take a temporary detour from the mainstem and leave Henrietta as she continues on up the Mattole River.

## WILDER RIDGE

Before we travel up the road that is on the ridge between Honeydew Creek and the river, and snake along on switchbacks until eventually flattening out on top of the ridge, I'll pause at the base of the mountain and present you with a picture of what used to be called The Upside-down Bridge. It has always been fun traveling with strangers to Wilder Ridge road for their very first trip. When approaching this Honeydew Creek crossing, folks would point and exclaim, "Oh, look. They put the bridge in upside-down!" But no, it was installed that way on purpose.

I included this photo of the bridge for a good reason. It's history now, and was replaced in the late summer of 1989. The new bridge has a straighter alignment with the road and is a two lane concrete structure. I've noticed people turning this picture of the upside-down bridge upside-down to look at it. It still looks funny.

Almost immediately after crossing the new rightside-up bridge, the second tributary to Honeydew Creek flows under the road. This stream is called High Prairie Creek, because of the open grasslands in its headwaters. This watershed is about as stable as a bowl of jelly sitting on a washing machine set on the spin cycle. One of these days a huge debris slide will flush a lot of history down the tubes.

Let's continue up the switchbacks of Wilder Ridge to review some more history.

In 1880, Dave Conover had a trading post up on Wilder Ridge. John Randolph Fox, and his adopted son, Davy Wright, also took up residency here. A ridge dropping down into Honeydew Creek was named after Davy Wright. Mr. Wright later left this ridge and became a blacksmith in Petrolia.

Many times while traveling over this ridge I have wondered about the name. It's called Wilder Ridge. Had anyone named Wilder ever lived here? Sure enough, I was rescued by the 1860 census once again. It told me that Daniel Wilder departed from Massa-

*The Upside-down Bridge over Honeydew Creek has been replaced by a new one that is wider and aligned straighter with the road that heads up Wilder Ridge.*

chusetts to come west. He left the sea breeze of the Atlantic to eventually settle here where he could enjoy the sea breeze of the Pacific. So, thanks to his wanderings, we are using this title today. When I discovered that twenty-five years later Sanford Wilder married Jeannie Piner, the title of Wilder Ridge was further confirmed.

## FOX SPRING
If you look at a map of Wilder Ridge hoping to find Fox Spring, you probably won't. As previously mentioned, John Randolph Fox dwelt in this area. This spring, located near the top of the ridge, was a watering hole for wagon teams in the early days.

Getting a little nostalgic, let me tell you how I know about this. My dad was an avid baseball fan.

We learned of a picnic and ball game in Ettersburg. He had the horse and wagon ready to roll at four o'clock in the morning. A child four or five years old, as I was at the time, needed a place to sleep in the bed of the wagon. I remember curling up in the pile of hay which was put there for those who needed rest. As close as I can remember, it was approximately noon when we arrived, and after the ball game and festivities, it was long after dark before we returned home. I remember my mother asking if we were going to stop at Fox Spring to water the horses. I watched carefully while approaching, during the watering, and while leaving, but was extremely disappointed when I never encountered one darn fox!

Near the summit along Wilder Ridge Road is the junction with Horse Mountain Road that bears off to the west, crosses South Fork Bear Creek, and continues on eventually to Shelter Cove. This road was constructed in 1876. Its primary use in those days was for the transport of salt from sailing ships to the many stock ranches in the territory.

## AB CREEK

Any fish continuing past Honeydew Creek will shortly come to a small feeder stream collecting its water from topography on the southwest side of the river known as the Ab. Now, we've always referred to abalone as abs, but this property is so far removed from the ocean that the idea was too silly to consider as a possibility. Therefore, I was happy to learn from my research that Absalom Gudom came to this particular area in 1881 to take up residency. Sometime later he moved into Petrolia proper and opened a livery stable.

Let me make a few comments at this time concerning the way that names get changed or lost completely. Historical landmark names sometimes get changed by newcomers to an area. Such is the case here where a creek without a name across the river from the Ab is being referred to as Ab Creek by new residents. If it were at all possible to communicate with Mr. Absalom Gudom, I'm sure he would testify that the stream originating from his property on the southwest side, was, and is, Ab Creek.

In 1983, a fish such as Henrietta would have encountered something new about a half mile upstream of Ab Creek. A gigantic landslide dropped into the Mattole River and entirely blocked the channel. The slide debris forced the river into the Ab's west bank, which in turn began to fall into the river. With all of this material entering the channel, a lake forty feet deep was created. The river eventually washed away most of the mud and gravel, and only very large boulders lagged behind to form a cascade, which presents no problem for fish migration.

## BIG GULCH

Our historical progress now moves us upstream a couple miles where Henrietta might observe a large gorge in the mountainside to the southwest known as Big Gulch. This area should be referred to as canyonland supreme. It was while writing of this particular landscape that I suddenly realized why the pioneers built the wagon road on top of Wilder Ridge instead of along the valley floor.

## PRINGLE RIDGE

On the southeast side of Big Gulch is a major ridgeline which provides us with the old pioneer name of Pringle. Pringle Ridge was used as a major pack trail route by early settlers.

## DRY CREEK

The information bucket was nearly dry when Henrietta approached this neighborhood. Most creeks, as you have noticed by now, acquired titles as a result of the people who lived adjacent to them. It would be futile, though, to assume that anyone named Dry lived here. Checking with residents in this section, I learned that Henrietta could possibly find a suitable spawning bed in the lower part of the creek; however, depending upon the water flow, there are occasions when the creek runs underground. I had just finished writing these lines when I had a visit from an old-timer. As he perused this page he exclaimed, "That's not the name of that creek!" I asked, "Well, what is it then?" "I don't know," he said soberly, "but I know that's not it!" How's that for dry humor?

## MIDDLE CREEK

We've finally caught up with Henrietta. Her slippery body now glides by Dry Creek as she angles her fins for an upstream course through the whirlpools of the turbulently flowing Mattole, and finds herself at yet another stream entering the river. This is Middle Creek. This stream once bore a different name. As you may remember, this book began with a conversation between myself and Joe Erwin. In the headwaters of Middle Creek, the Erwin family were residents during the early days. At that time in history, Middle Creek was known as Erwin Creek.

To confuse the issue, might I say that much of the water running into this creek apparently comes from Middle Ridge. More water flows from the slopes of Stewart Ridge. As usual, I looked at my old maps of this area, and found that E. L. Stewart lived here in 1898. Whether we call it Middle Creek, Erwin Creek, or Stewart Creek, Henrietta couldn't care less, and she moves on upstream.

## WESTLUND CREEK

Dropping into the Mattole from the same direction, we come to Westlund Creek. Here again a name change nearly came about. Mapmakers, while working in this area, decided that this creek should be named for the folks who were living there. These people honestly informed the mapmakers that the Westlunds inhabited the area before they did. So it became Westlund Creek.

## GILHAM CREEK

Henrietta's natural instinct tells her spawning time is drawing near. She now swiftly moves upstream. So shall we. We will only take time at this location to explain that Mr. Gilham came to this area to work for Mr. Scott. While Mr. Scott was prominent enough to have a homestead (as shown on some old maps) and employ Mr. Gilham, apparently he wasn't prominent enough to have a creek and a butte named after him, as was Mr. Gilham.

## DUNCAN CREEK/DUNCAN FLAT/DUNCAN PREEMPTION

The origin of these three titles is due to an individual named Charles Duncan. The flat and the creek are more or less self-explanatory, but a few words about preemptions may be helpful.

The Duncans had settled along the Mattole very early. They had what is called a preemption, which was a form of land ownership before deeds were used. The first preemption was acquired in 1868. By 1882 there were nearly 5000 such land registrations countywide. A startling fact just crossed my mind. In 1850 only Indians roamed the Mattole. Thirty-two years later white settlers had claimed an awful lot of territory.

In theory, a preemption was like a bird roosting on a limb in a tree. "This is my tree," he calls out, and all other birds respect his claim and stay away. Then comes the government with its restrictions and regulations. Today, it is nearly down to the point where a bird would nearly need a permit to set in his own tree. Wasn't life simpler for the Duncans?

## FOURMILE CREEK

When Hen comes to the next creek on the west side of the river, she is in a big rush now and goes right on by it without even giving it a glance. I only wish that I could have done the same.

For the first time in writing these pages, I must face defeat. Did you ever come up against a stone wall and find no opening? I was told that the creek was four miles long and thus the title. WRONG! It is neither four miles long, nor four miles from anyplace like Ettersburg, for instance, nor is it four miles from anywhere. Well, actually it is four miles from somewhere.

## PHRONIE'S FLAT
After leaving Fourmile Creek, our aquatic friend has a couple miles to swim before reaching the next landmark. As I was anxious to put space between myself and Fourmile Creek, I'll move ahead of Henrietta to Phronie's Flat.

There are two unnamed ephemeral creeks that descend from the northeast slopes about a quarter mile apart. In between them is a small peak, and directly behind this peak is a grassy opening called Phronie's Flat. Here I lucked out again. I interviewed an old-timer in his nineties who remembered Sephronia Hunter, Phronie for short. Her father, Judge Hunter (remember Hunter Bluff?) had vast land holdings is this region.

## BUCKEYE RIDGE
Once again we have a duplicate name for a ridge near Phronie's Flat. A very ancient gentleman told me he remembered many Buckeye trees growing in this area.

## RAIL PILE RIDGE
This landmark is a tad more interesting than the last one. Before the days of barbed wire and staples, pioneers built fences from rails. These rails were split from logs. The settler who enclosed his pasture here with a split rail fence either arrived before barbed wire, or simply liked the old ways better.

Unfortunately, I was unable to learn his name, but I did learn from the same old-timer who gave me the insight about Buckeye Ridge that he personally remembered seeing that split rail fence when he was a small boy.

## SHOLES CREEK

Across the river from Rail Pile Ridge is Sholes Creek. The history of this creek was simple to uncover because Mr. Orville Sholes was my neighbor when I began writing this book. The Sholes homesteaded property along this creek in 1912, and Orville was raised on the land there. The Belcher Abstract and Title Company map in the County Recorders office shows that Daisy K. Sholes was living in the headwaters of Sholes Creek in 1921.

Henrietta, unfortunately, would not have the same opportunity to spawn in this creek as did her ancestors before logging. Spawning access was blocked by many log jams.

An interesting note regarding the original surveys that were performed in the Mattole will perhaps give you a chuckle. When the lines were surveyed around the vicinity of Sholes Creek, the man with the compass rode a horse. When his travel became too difficult for horseback, the rest of the measurement was simply guessed at. Much later, when more modern instruments were used to resurvey the territory, the original lines were found to be reasonably close — only a quarter mile off.

## HARROW CREEK

Henrietta has continued on up the river and as we follow her we pass by a small tributary on the west side known as Harrow Creek. This low gradient basin was settled early by Asa Harrow who, as documented in the 1860 census, came west from Virginia. The Harrow family sank very deep roots. Coupled with a love of the land and pioneer persistence, the Harrows still own land there today.

## GRINDSTONE CREEK

As Henrietta zig-zags on upstream, she searches for the perfect gravel, cleanest water, and safest spot to lay her eggs. She bypasses Grindstone Creek, which enters the river from the northeast. Her ancestral instinct warns her of an incident which took place up that creek a long time ago. I interviewed a gentleman who was nearly a hundred years old. Charlie Hacker told me he heard this story when he was a very small boy. During the period when wagon trains began to travel the ridges, a heavily laden wagon lost a large grindstone which was not securely tied down. It rolled, and rolled, and rolled. Eventually, it splashed into the creek, nearly scaring the scales off of several salmon resting there.

Another possibility for the origin of this stream's name was passed on to me by a respectable landowner who lived nearby. The Indians of the area used this location to grind acorns into flour. Many of these grinding stones were left behind and discovered by later residents. Now, you are left with two choices for the origin of this creek's name. Take your pick.

Before leaving Grindstone Creek, I feel I should mention the Hunter Place. There were few residents during Judge Hunter's stay among these hills, although he did have occasional visitors to his homestead, who used the nearby pack trail on their way into the Mattole Valley. There was a school house near Grindstone Creek, but there were not enough children to meet the legally required number of pupils. Seven-year-old Charlie Hacker came to live with the Hunter family. It was his registration at the school which met the necessary attendance quota.

Charlie, already a good horseman at seven, rode to Shelter Cove with a large pack train. At the cove they would wait for a ship to come in and unload salt. The pack animals would be loaded with the salt and then climb the hills and return to the Mattole with enough of the valuable mineral for another year's livestock supply.

While waiting for the ship to arrive, little Charlie investigated his surroundings as any curious child might do. One target of his curiosity was a large pile of bones. He was found entertaining himself in this bone pile and his back pockets were roughly dusted off! Many, many moons ago a great battle had taken place on these premises between the original inhabitants and the encroachers. Charlie was found playing with the remains of the unfortunate losers.

## STERRIT HOLE

In 1868 the Marysville Settlers found an impassable situation in their journey along the Mattole Valley. They faced a narrow rock chasm with water too swift and deep for their wagons to negotiate. This gorge had to be avoided by the wagon train. Frank and William Sterrit, settlers in this vicinity, were skeptical of the hazard created by the narrow passage. One day, Frank attempted to ride his horse through the treacherous waters of the gorge, and was drowned. Ever since that time in 1875, and now more than a century later, it is still referred to as Sterrit Hole. There must be a better way to gain notoriety than by drowning, but unfortunately, as we have seen so far in our progress upstream, this is all too commonly the situation.

During my research of historical documents, I found a clipping that referred to the Sterrit Hotel. Two mistakes were made: one was Frank's fearless ride through the gorge, and the other was the newspaper that converted the word hole, into hotel. At any rate, Frank checked out.

## DOODYVILLE

On the ridge between Grindstone Creek and the next one upstream, Mattole Canyon Creek, there was an old settlement called Doodyville. Mike Doody and his brother William and their large families took up residence here by 1921 and were shortly joined by enough other people to create a small community. Not all old-time settlements flourished into a megalopolis. This one certainly didn't because there are about the same number of residents in that particular location now as originally— just a handful. However, the surrounding neighborhood is loaded with newcomers. The road that leads past this old settlement is still called Doodyville Road, although some newcomers have taken to spelling it Dutyville instead. Henrietta has no interest in this controversy. Her duty is to procreate, so she glides through the current to investigate Mattole Canyon Creek.

## MATTOLE CANYON CREEK

Because the wide mouth of Mattole Canyon Creek is about as far from being a canyon as possible, we have to assume that the name originated because of the nature of the Mattole River itself, which is canyonlike both above and below the confluence.

Anyone passing through this region might ask about the origin of the name Crooked Prairie, located along the south ridge partway up the creek. Well, believe it or not, it has a simple explanation. This grassland takes the form of a giant lopsided horseshoe, and someone aptly named it as they saw it.

If Henrietta detected a strange scent at the mouth of Mattole Canyon Creek, it is quite possible she smelled the unique essence of cedar. Raking my mind, I could conjure up no other stream in the Mattole where native incense cedar trees grow in such abundance as they do here. During large freshets, cones have washed down from Cedar Flat in the headwaters and taken root along the creek.

Further up in the headwaters of this creek, Henrietta's ancestors may have detected another kind of scent, something like fertilizer, draining off from Elk Ridge. I met an old-timer who had roamed these hills as a youngster. He spoke of the countless elk that once lived here, and of the many antlers and skeletal bones from the great herds.

The law of 1873 forbidding men to shoot elk leaves me to believe that the politicians acted too slowly to save the helpless critters in this locale. As I look back in history to that time, I see that there was very little restraint for someone shooting an Indian, but killing an elk landed you in the slammer for two years. This might lead one to believe that it was better to have been an elk than an Indian.

## CLARK'S BUTTE

Here is a good example of how hard it is to do the research necessary in order to document the origin of a name.

    I talked to T. K. Clark about this location and he gave me an answer in the negative. None of his early pioneer family had roots near Clark's Butte.

    I called and wrote many people who had lived in the vicinity to no avail. Many had arrived too late on the scene to be of any help.

    I made one last attempt to turn up an answer just before this page went to press, and took another trip to the County Recorder's Office. There I had help poring over scores of thick land patent books, looking up every Clark in the county, and the parcel locations. I found several within ten to twenty miles away, but none in the immediate vicinity. With a feeling of resignation I paged through one last book. Success was mine! There was David Clark. Homestead Certificate #665 was issued to him by President Chester A. Arthur on August 15, 1884. "Pursuant to the Act of Congress approved 20th May, 1862, TO SECURE HOMESTEADS TO ACTUAL SETTLERS ON THE PUBLIC DOMAIN," David Clark was granted 160 acres saddling Elk Ridge a short distance northwest of the peak now called Clark's Butte.

# ORIGIN OF MATTOLE

This is still pretty remote and rugged terrain! I imagine him hauling all his provisions to his homestead on the ridge with great difficulty, and his horse team dragging a heavily laden wagon up a rutted ridge. If horses talked to each other (and who is to say they don't), I can just picture the conversation as they profusely sweated up the mountainside. "Hey Dobbin, I wish old Clark would put this trip off a hundred years until he could get a four-wheel-drive wagon."

## BLUE SLIDE CREEK

After swimming forty-two miles so far, Henrietta has literally passed up dozens of little gulches and unnamed creeks on her way to the headwaters. Most of these have never been given a name, and if they have, I was unable to ferret out the information. There are some landmarks one can find very little to comment about, such as Blue Slide Creek. Why is it called Blue Slide Creek? If you found yourself within the walls of this canyon, you would readily understand the origin of the name. It has an overabundance of landslides. The decomposing shale becomes blue clay that is scientifically referred to among expert geologists as blue goo.

## GREEK TURN

After passing Blue Slide Creek there is a good possibility that Henrietta's vision will become clearer. Approximately a quarter mile ahead she will find another shadow across the river. It is a picturesque location where all fish find a place to rest for awhile. This little cement bridge carrying the county road was constructed in 1928. It replaced a wooden bridge that spanned the river no further than a quail's call downstream. The contractor for the original wooden bridge hired a crew of Greek immigrants. A communication barrier between the workers and the contractor resulted in many problems. The gaggle of mixed language indelibly etched a mark in the memory of local residents. At this writing, that first curve up the mountainside east of Ettersburg is still known as the Greek Turn.

## BEAR CREEK

All this bridge talk is just Greek to Henrietta so she moves on upstream to Bear Creek, which meets the Mattole River near downtown Ettersburg. As you may remember, there is more than one Bear Creek. The twenty-two square miles of this tributary drainage constitute the third largest in the Mattole watershed, fifteen miles in length. It drains the central and southern slopes of the King Range. Important tributaries of Bear Creek are French Creek, Jewett Creek, North Fork Bear, and South Fork Bear.

Everyone agreed that there were too many bear existing along this stream. Bear, like humans, enjoyed a fish dinner, and old Smokey could wade out in the creek and swat a fat salmon out of the water and onto the beach. This is wild and remote country. There is enough rugged terrain along this creek for a good population of bear to reside, and the name is likely to pass on for many future generations.

French Creek joins the Bear not far from the Mattole River. The land around this juncture has been in the French family for generations. After speaking with Lee French and Ralph French I have no problem designating the title of this creek to their family tree.

Another resident of French Creek was Fred Farnsworth, who was introduced early in the book. He told me of a visit he made to his neighbors one fine day, and of the strange and surprising events that occurred. As he approached their farm, he heard squawking from the chicken house. His neighbor's wife was probing the interior of the shed with a long pole. She was trying to roust their pig, who had invaded the chicken's domain. Suddenly, the porker took the hint that he was not wanted in there, and charged out the door right between the woman's legs. She fell upon the pig's back, grabbed it by the tail, and hung on for dear life as two hundred pounds of ham ran squealing for the river. Each time I tried to get Fred to tell me the outcome of the story, he got to laughing so hard that I never did hear the ending.

Bear Creek has been a haven for many runs of salmon. The Indians enjoyed a rich fish harvest during their stay in this area. Should any salmon become spooked by the human's harvesting plans, they could move a mile and a half upstream to a safer location at Jewett Creek. Now, you are wondering about Jewett Creek. I have in my hand as I write this a copy of an old deed dated October 6, 1881, conferring title for 120 acres of land in this locality to Charles W. Jewett.

# 13

# ETTERSBURG TO WHITETHORN

## ETTERSBURG

I would like to begin this paragraph by speaking of the town of Ettersburg. But, the post office is gone, the store is gone, and the five-hundred goat dairy is gone. What is left of Ettersburg proper lies between Bear Creek and the county road, just west of the Mattole River, and is basically the French's ranch.

    A very famous man once lived here. His name was Albert Felix Etter, and he was born in 1872. He became the north coast's leading horticulturist, and was nearly as well-known as Luther Burbank. During his lifetime, he cross-pollinated many trees and other kinds of plants. I so admire Mr. Etter's green thumb. When I enter my garden, my plants all tremble and shiver at the appearance of my two brown thumbs.

    Henrietta is tired of swimming. If she had a

thumb, she would probably stick it out for a ride into the next chapter. But, before we leave this area, let me describe an incident that took place in the days when all men who ventured west came toting rifles. If you had a disagreeable neighbor, he was often dispatched with lead, that is, if one was a fair shot. The story I'm about to relate took place on Wilder Ridge one early morning. The intended target walked out of his barn and was fired upon by a bushwhacker hiding behind a small tree a short distance away. The victim ran back into the barn and peered out through a knothole. All he could locate was the sniper's posterior sticking out from behind the tree. It was the best target he could find, and being an excellent marksman, he fired his piece and cut a groove across the back pockets. MORAL: Should you ever wish to attack an enemy in this manner, make darn sure you pick a tree large enough to hide your buns.

## WOLF CREEK

Henrietta will not travel far up the Mattole before she encounters a stream trickling in from the east. Once upon a time it was called Box Canyon Creek, but now it is referred to as Wolf Creek. This stream gathers rainfall from the Wolf Ranch. No, no one raises wolves here. The Wolf family has raised sheep on their acreage for many decades, though.

Fred Wolf told me that in all the years they gathered woollies on their property, they never encountered a rattlesnake. Then, one winter when some youngsters were playing around on the ranch, a rattler was discovered by them under a large rock.

Before their exploration ended that day, they had located over sixty hibernating rattlesnakes in a den. Downstream on the Miner Ranch, as you remember, we have never come face to fang with those poisonous vipers. But, I'll tell you, after that discovery of buzz tails on the Wolf Ranch, I find myself more vigilant when hiking through the hills where I live. In fact, of late I've been known to jump several feet from the buzz of a grasshopper.

## LITTLE FINLEY CREEK AND BIG FINLEY CREEK

Now we will return to Hen as she snakes along through the current toward the next tributary entering the Mattole River from the west bank. At this point, she'll swim by Little Finley Creek, and within a half mile further along on the same side she'll pass by Big Finley Creek. There were tragic times regarding the settlers of this area. The exact nature of the difficulties is uncertain, but according to the information passed on to me, the Finley family departed from the territory abruptly, leaving only their name to the creeks.

## EUBANKS CREEK

My information concerning this landmark came to me from one of my many visits to Fred Farnsworth. Caleb William "Billy" Eubanks once lived here in a log cabin. The location was approximately a mile up the creek from the Mattole River. After the departure of the Eubanks family, Fred said that the Farnsworth family spent some time here, and made some improvements to the holdings.

The source of water for Eubanks Creek comes from Telegraph Ridge, which is the eastern watershed boundary between the Mattole and Eel River valleys. Unlike the previously mentioned Telegraph Ridge or Peak, this Telegraph Ridge actually did have telegraph wires that ran along it to service Ettersburg. Insulators that were attached to trees were harvested by loggers who cut timber along the ridge over a half century later.

## NOONING CREEK

Henrietta likes to nose around the mouth of each stream as it enters the river. Once again she swings over to the west bank to examine the next creek as it splashes into the Mattole.

Most maps you will encounter title this stream Nooning Creek. My knowledge of the derivation of this name came about through a conversation with my father. He told me that he had been a teamster on the road from Briceland to Shelter Cove. On the highest ridge between the Mattole River and the crossing at South Fork Bear Creek was a level spot where most of the wagon jockeys ate lunch while their animals rested. It was commonly known as the Nooning Grounds, and old maps even locate that spot as such. On the north side of this ridge, runoff enters Nooning Creek. Believe it or not, as I write this, an old map hangs on my wall that denotes this stream as "NOONER CREEK." This leads me to wonder exactly what activities this particular mapmaker was engaged in during his lunch break. There is humor in this question, and should you not be old enough to understand it, refer to one of your elders for the answer.

## SINKYONE CREEK
If many of Henrietta's elders were apprehensive about this next waterway, they surely had a bonafide excuse for bypassing it. The large flat at the mouth of this creek, on the north side of the river, was a major encampment of the Sinkyone Indians. When either salmon or venison finds its way onto my plate, I realize the Indians didn't have it all that tough.

## BRIDGE CREEK
Henrietta finds another shadow on the water. She is a descendant of many thousands of other salmon who preceded her past this location, and I'm not

*This early morning view looks east out over fog-shrouded Ettersburg Valley.*

certain at what point in history the first fish found a shadow on the water caused by a bridge. However, I clearly remember the existing structure being built in 1971. When Frankie Lawrence and I were on our way to Shelter Cove to find some abalone, we were held up by workmen on the bridge, and nearly missed the low tide. As Hen passes under the bridge, she immediately encounters a creek of sizable proportions on the south bank. "Guess what, Hen? This one's called Bridge Creek."

For such a simple name, its history is more complicated than it seems. When timber was taken from this watershed it was called Hoist Creek because logs had to be lifted vertically out of the canyon. This type of operation wasn't economically lucrative and may have led to its later naming as Hungry Gulch. Sometime during early history it was known as Adams Creek, but for obvious reasons was later named Bridge Creek. Interestingly enough, the old map I referred to earlier shows that the main portion of the creek was called Robinson Creek. An old-timer assured me there really was a Robinson family in existence in this locale, and he had visited them many times.

## KING RANGE

The mental strain encountered in the last paragraph would surely tire fish and human minds alike. Henrietta opts to take a rest while we take a short detour westward on the road to Shelter Cove. Once we leave the Mattole River, and travel along the road that traverses the ridge between Bridge Creek and Nooning Creek, we come to the Nooning Grounds flat previously mentioned. After descending the western slope of this ridge, we eventually arrive at the bottom, and cross South Fork Bear Creek at a point approximately two miles from its headwaters. Much of the flow entering these headwaters of South Fork Bear Creek pours in from the eastern slopes of a ridge mapped by the U.S.G.S. as Chamisal Mountain. The Bureau of Land Management maps spell the name a little differently and refer to Chemise Mountain. At any rate, the peak of this ridgeline tops out at nearly 2,600 feet, and is locally spoken of as Chamise Mountain. I was a little confused whether to refer to this mountain as Chamise or Chamisal. My *Encyclopedia Britannica* helped me out here. It said, "Chamise is the most abundant and characteristic small shrub of the higher foothills west of the Sierra Nevada, where ... it often forms a distinct zone called chamisal."

Imagine yourself standing at the headwaters of South Fork Bear Creek and watching a Chamise leaf fall into the stream. If you were able to follow this leaf's progress, here is the route you would take. The leaf would lead you in a northerly direction away from Chamise Mountain. The leaf floats several miles before passing at the feet of the queen. In this case, I'm speaking of Queen Peak, which rises up east of South Fork Bear Creek, at the headwaters of Big Finley Creek, and stands at over 2,800 feet.

Within another couple creek miles the leaf floats along at the base of Paradise Ridge. This ridge runs north from Queen Peak about three miles, and forms the watershed boundary for Big and Little Finley Creeks off to the east. Fact or fiction, the story related to me is as follows. An early pioneer of

Ettersburg stood in his front yard one day and looked up at the western ridgelines, and exclaimed, "This view is paradise!" I find no fault with his view.

As the leaf continues, it passes Horse Mountain, which stands off to the west, like an island in the fog, at a little over 1,900 feet. Horse Mountain Ridge extends all the way from Horse Mountain to Saddle Mountain, which tops out at nearly 3,300 feet. I cannot honestly say that I know the exact reason for the naming of this mountain. However, it is self-evident that a person's pony played a part in the penning of the pinnacle.

Directly east of Saddle Mountain, the leaf encounters a strong southeasterly current of water that forces it on toward Ettersburg. This strong current is the North Fork of Bear Creek, and here, the two forks merge into Bear Creek proper. At this point, let's leave the leaf to leisurely drift on downstream while we return to the ridge to ride the range.

This entire region of ridges and peaks is called the King Range. I already mentioned Queen Peak, and every queen should have a king. North of Saddle Mountain is King Peak, for which the range was named.

The search for the story behind the entitlement of King Peak gave me one royal headache! I expected to find an early settler named King, or at least an account of someone conferring kingly dignity to this monarch parting the clouds at 4,088 feet. This abrupt rise, occurring less than three miles from the ocean, is rare along the coast of California, or for that matter, anywhere along coastlines throughout the world.

When I couldn't find any records of old-timers

named King who lived in the vicinity, I began to think perhaps very early explorers named the mountain. Some of the earliest explorers were the Spanish who sailed up the coast of North America claiming and naming for the king of Spain.

A prominent peak like this one would surely have been noticed by the likes of Juan Rodriguez Cabrillo,

*Looking south from atop Cooskie Mountain, the majestic King Range fills the view.*

who discovered and named Cape Mendocino on February 26, 1543. King Phillip II aspired to the Spanish throne in 1556 and commissioned intensive exploration of the California coast that continued for almost two centuries. I thought perhaps I'd find an old Spanish map claiming King Peak, but after reviewing many very old maps, I never saw it mentioned.

Leafing through the pages of history, I had trouble getting past 1898, where in the Clark Museum in Eureka an old map clearly delineates King Peak. Gibbes map of California from 1852 made no mention of King Peak or any other peak in northern California, or even of Humboldt County itself for that matter! The Germans got one better on us with a very detailed map of California entitled *Karte Von Californien* published in 1849, and even though it made no mention of King Peak, it did name Mount Diablo. In 1853, John B. Trask's *Topographical Map of the Mineral Districts of California* was lithographed and published by Britton and Rey of San Francisco. "Being the first map ever published from actual survey," I had great hopes it would shed some light on the subject. Interestingly enough, the King Range mountains were shown, and King Peak was drawn in, but it wasn't labeled.

Thanks to the United States Coast and Geodetic Survey who published the work, I was able to push a confirmed date for the name of King Peak back to 1889. George Davidson thoroughly depicted the King Range and King Peak, both in sketches and names, as well as a multitude of other geographic features of the North Coast, in his masterpiece known as the *Pacific Coast - Coast Pilot*. In 1850, he was a member of the first party sent by the U.S. Coast Survey to chart the Pacific Coast. I'd love to get a look at some of Davidson's preliminary notes.

So who was King? Some people have suggested it might have been Clarence Rivers King who worked for the U.S. Geologic Survey early on, and from 1867 to 1878 conducted a famous exploration of the 40th parallel. I went to the library and looked at a book he had written about his expedition. I was excited to see references in the index to Humboldt Mountains, and King Peak! At last, I thought, and then broke out in laughter when it turned out the Humboldt Mountains referred to were in Nevada, and the mountain named King Peak was in Antarctica! Later I found out Utah's highest mountain standing at 13,528 feet, called King Peak, was also named after Clarence. Interestingly enough, further inquiry indicated he probably never even set foot in Humboldt County. But, another King certainly influenced what happened here.

The federal *Appropriations Act of March 3, 1851* provided for a Surveyor General of California, and on March 24, 1851, Samuel D. King was appointed to the position. He was in charge of conducting the rectangular survey of California and succeeded in establishing the three initial baseline and meridian points of Mount Diablo in 1851, San Bernardino in 1852, and the Humboldt District in 1853. On October 6, 1853, Deputy Surveyor Henry Washington established the initial point of the Humboldt Meridian on the summit of Mount Pierce.

In the *Records of the General Land Office Report of Deputy Surveyor Henry Washington to Surveyor General for California* dated 11/8/1853, Washington writing back to his boss said: "I ventured to Humboldt Bay and examined the country around it thoroughly, likewise the country to the East and South towards Eel River finally fixed upon a very prominent mountain peak on the dividing ridge between Eel and Bear Rivers as the initial point for the Base and Meridian lines. It has been named Mount Pierce as a compliment to the President, and the monument, with the materials furnished from your office, was erected on said mountain peak on the 6th of October 1853." It is interesting to note that President Franklin Pierce was elected to office in 1853, and Washington enjoyed complimenting that authority by naming the Monument Peak after him. Washington closed his letter with the salutation: "I am with great respect your obedient servant."

The Humboldt Meridian line runs south from Mount Pierce directly to King Peak and Washington made reference to the peak that is accurate both in terms of distance and elevation. This strongly suggests that Samuel King's obedient servant, Mr. Washington, did his boss the honors of bestowing the title for him. After the initial point was established, many years passed with very few surveys conducted in the Humboldt District because of the remote and rugged terrain. The Surveyor General couldn't get deputies to contract for surveys there at the price allowed by law, which was $15 per mile.

This explanation may not satisfy some readers, but it is more plausible than many other stories kicking around the countryside. For instance, I was informed that Kaluna Cliff, just west of Queen Peak, was named for King Kaluna of the Hawaiian Islands, as was King Peak. In fact, the name was derived from a Sandwich Island brig named the *Kaluna* which went ashore directly under the cliff. The timber aboard was only partially salvaged due to a large landslide that covered it up.

Another wild goose chase led briefly past current generations of King surnames who claimed lineage without offering any convincing proof. Somewhere along the line the original name of King Peak got corrupted into King's Peak. One author who wrote a book on place names used this distorted moniker, with an incorrect elevation for the mountain, and even attributed the title to some unknown captain of the U.S. Army.

Any further information coming my way will be digested for revision in future printings. For now, I can feel that royal headache easing, and at any rate, the monarch of this coastal mountain range is well deserving of its title.

For those readers who have not studied geology, you may find the following few words of interest concerning the next landmark, North Slide Peak, which is located on the ridge about four miles northwest of King Peak.

Wait! Did you feel that? My house is trembling. If you are reading this at a location within a hundred miles from me, you probably just experienced the same shake I just felt. Frequent earthquakes are an all too common occurrence on the north coast of California. Here in the Mattole, quakes result in the constant uplift of the King Range. It is the most seismically active region in North America, because it's in the vicinity of three tectonic plates jamming together. The topography of the North Slide Peak area bears witness to the upheaval caused by activity of this triple junction. Standing on top of this mountain, at over 3,500 feet, one can overlook the Pacific Ocean, or can look north into the headwaters of Squaw Creek, or east into the headwaters of Honeydew Creek.

While we are on the subject of earthquakes, you may get a chuckle out of this tale. A gentleman I knew had been ailing for a very long time, and the day finally came for his passing. At a family gathering a few days later, the group lamenting his death was interrupted by a strong seismic thump. Two members of the grieving party looked up and exclaimed in unison, "Well, he got there!"

The tremor I just experienced most likely vibrated the river bottom at Bridge Creek, and you-know-who is suddenly ready to move rapidly upstream. If we want to continue on with our companion, we best rejoin her now.

With a few wiggles of her tail, Henrietta leaves her resting place at Bridge Creek, arrives at the next creek, and zips on by. We shouldn't move past this next creek as fast as she did, although it is tempting because of its ambiguity.

## PAINTER CREEK AND MCKEE CREEK

When I interviewed an elder resident of this vicinity, the information I was given was based on supposition. "I suppose," he said, "you've heard the song of Davy Crockett who `killed him a bar, when he was only three.'" Well, many folks came west with a southern drawl as long as a wagon tongue. The word panther, drawn out, can sound like painter. More convincing yet was a map I found published in 1973, from a state agency studying the Mattole watershed. Painter Creek was clearly labeled as Panther Creek. However, upon doing more research I located a map from 1898 that showed L. Painter lived in this neck of the woods.

What is more mind-boggling is McKee Creek. Only a hop, skip, and a jump from the Mattole River, Painter is joined by McKee. But wait, it could be that McKee Creek is joined by Painter Creek. It all depends on the individual you put the question to. Which one is a tributary to the other one is anybody's guess. Personally, I would tend to lean toward the McKee title for the primary creek, because the McKee family name is by far the more prominent. Don Alonzo McKee, a fifty-two-year-old farmer from New York, registered to vote at Thorn on June 1, 1896. The McKees have been here ever since.

## VANARKIN CREEK

As Henrietta passes Vanarkin Creek (the next one she comes to, from the east) she is not too many miles from the headwaters of the Mattole. The Vanarkin family lived on a large flat along this creek. This is all I could find concerning this family, but an interesting story popped up as I was making inquiries. An early entrepreneur learned that split posts were in great demand for building stock fences on the ranchlands around Petrolia. After making several hundred posts, he lashed these together and prepared to raft them down the river during the first freshet. Unfortunately, the raft did not get far before it fell apart. Henrietta's ancestors, swimming upstream, met the posts heading downstream. Dodging fence posts at every turn in the river would not make for a happy salmon, but the ranchers in the lower river were delighted to rescue the wayward posts. I'd be willing to bet these were top quality products, drawn from the heart of the redwood tree. Speaking of red hearts, I nearly forgot to mention that the Valentine family had a ranch on this stream located near the mouth. In fact, Vanarkin has been known in some circles as Valentine Creek.

## ANDERSON CREEK
Huh? Nobody in Whitethorn could tell me anything about the origin of the name. If Henrietta knows, she isn't talking. However, deep in the archives I eventually came up with the following information.

Andrew Anderson was a woodsman in Thorn in 1896. Records show that he was thirty-four years old, five foot five inches tall, of fair complexion, with blue eyes and brown hair. He even had a scar on his left cheek. His native country was Finland, and he could read the Constitution in the English language as well as being able to write his name. All of this information was supplied by the Voter Precinct Register for Whitethorn of that year. What the Register does not report is what divine power drew this man from his native country, all the way across the sea, to this remote valley of very few people.

## UPPER MILL CREEK
This is the last Mill Creek that Henrietta will pass. This one is somewhat different than the last three previously mentioned. The reason for this is that Burt McKee, who operated the sawmill here, pro-

duced railroad ties. None of the others did. These ties were destined for use on the railroad line between Bear Harbor and Piercy. It's interesting to note that the Mattole River has four Mill Creeks, but no mills operate on them today.

## HARRIS CREEK

This was an easy one. Any longtime resident of this area remembers that Alfred Harris built the first store near the mouth of this creek. It became the hub of the community now known as Whitethorn.

# 14

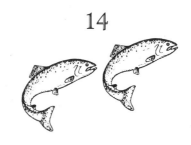

# WHITETHORN TO THE HEADWATERS

## WHITETHORN

Al Harris didn't operate the store for long before it changed owners and the Lewis family became the new proprietors. Harold Lewis, a longtime resident of Whitethorn, and manager of his family's business, was very helpful in providing some interesting historical background.

Because of the abundance of a type of *Ceanothus* brush (whitethorn) in this locality, the origin of the town's name is quite understandable. The first settlement was actually called Thorn. It was located at the junction of Shelter Cove Road and the turnoff for Whitethorn, which wasn't yet established. This location is still referred to as Thorn Junction.

When Harold's folks took over the store there were seventeen logging camps in the vicinity. In those early days, the mailman delivered mail no more than twice a week. Lacking a post office, the lumbermen asked that any mail for them be left at the store. Each evening, the store would be crowded with workers looking for letters or packages addressed to them. Sometimes a special letter would not arrive as expected and later it would be discovered that it was sent by error to a town like Thornton, of which there are ten with that name nation wide. Anyone who looks at the index of U.S. cities in a copy of today's zip code directory will find twenty-three towns that start with the word "Thorn." It's no wonder then, that when the first official post office opened here, Whitethorn was chosen as the name rather than Thorn.

Another decision was that mail should be delivered daily. However, even though this was accomplished (remember that this was still in the days of the old coal oil lamps, inadequate lighting, and was pre-zip code), now a lot of mail ended up in Whitethorne, Virginia, way back on the east coast!

Today as I write this, in 1996, the store at Whitethorn is closed, and the post office has been relocated along the Shelter Cove road slightly west of Thorn Junction. Is this strange, or not? Thorn to Whitethorn, Whitethorn back to Thorn, but yet still Whitethorn! Some people hold out for the earlier name of Thorn. The fire station near the crossroads of Thorn Junction is still called Thorn Station.

## GIBSON CREEK AND GIBSON RIDGE

Henrietta has struggled nearly fifty-seven miles upstream since entering the Mattole, and now arrives at the mouth of Gibson Creek. This creek is about a quarter mile from Harris Creek, and enters the Mattole from the east side at the southern end of Whitethorn.

Gibson Ridge runs north-south along the eastern Mattole watershed divide, and provides runoff for several east slope creeks both upstream and downstream of Gibson Creek.

I interviewed a few old-timers, but I guess they weren't old enough. No one could add to my historical knowledge concerning Mr. Gibson. Once again, I resumed my quest for answers by referring to old documents, books, and maps. Jackpot! I finally found Mr. Gibson's history contained in a book in the courthouse. George C. Gibson owned at least 160 acres in this area in 1881, but I am not certain of the exact location where he put his feet under the table at dinner each night. Additionally, I found that Henry Brown Gibson lived in this proximity in 1896. He was listed in the Whitethorn Voters Precinct Register as a forty-six-year-old butcher from Iowa.

If I were to stand on the bank of the river and ask Hen which one of these gentlemen, George or Henry, deserves credit for the title of this little creek or the ridge, she would no doubt shake her head and swim on to Stanley Creek.

## STANLEY CREEK

Henrietta, in half a mile, finds herself at the mouth of Stanley Creek. She only remains long enough for us to learn that there was a man named Art Stanley who lived here. He used the flats adjacent to this creek for his base of operations. He produced redwood split products like fence posts, grape stakes, and shingle bolts. Mr. Stanley was only one of many entrepreneurs in this area turning out redwood products. But what was different about Art was that he had a creek named after him.

## BAKER CREEK

Baker Creek flows from Gibson Ridge, as do the other five previously mentioned creeks that enter from the east slopes. During the stagecoach era, accommodations at Baker Creek served weary travelers as a way station.

Once again, the Voter Registration of 1896 paid off. Henry Elsworth Baker was entered on the rolls as a farmer from Illinois. He was thirty-three years old at the time, five foot nine inches tall, with light complexion, blue eyes, and light colored hair. Since there were so few people in the vicinity, Henry wins the honors for the name of Baker Creek.

Hen passes up still another creek that offers suitable spawning ground because her natural instinct insists that she hasn't yet come to her ancestral spot. Still cautious, she can't afford to let her guard down now. Wary, and more than a bit weary, she rests awhile at the mouth of Baker Creek. She has dodged many enemies during her three years in the ocean. She skirted sea lions at the mouth, evaded bear who would have scooped her onto the bank for dinner, and outsmarted many men who tossed lures at her. Perhaps even an occasional gaff spear was jabbed her way, and yet she prevailed.

There is one danger that Hen luckily avoided simply by the fact that the threat no longer exists: the nets deployed by fish- hungry men in boats. When I was a very small lad, I remember watching a man in a boat drifting down the river by our place near Squaw Creek. This boatman held a rope attached to a long net, and accompanied by another man walking along the shore, they captured whatever salmon were in the waters. As the net filled up with fish they pulled it ashore. If they weren't satisfied with the quantity, they would repeat the process until they were. Henrietta lost many of her ancestors from this type of fishing in the early days.

Long before we notice it, Henrietta's inherent instinct warns her of an impending storm. With her built-in barometer, she senses rain clouds building, and hard south winds approaching. To what extent the rainfall will swell the river is a determining factor in Hen's next decision. Having left Baker Creek behind, she travels less than a half mile, when she crosses the county line.

It is an interesting fact that the Klamath, Mad, and Eel Rivers all have something in common. The headwaters of each are in a different county than their respective main portions and mouths. As Hen crosses the county line from Humboldt into Mendocino, the Mattole River can now be added to this list.

It doesn't seem honorable to leave Humboldt County without tending to its origin. Humboldt County was created on March 12, 1853, from territory which previously had been a part of Trinity County. Its original boundaries were defined as follows.

"Commencing on the north at a point in the ocean three miles due west of the mouth of Mad

River; thence due east from the point of beginning to the Trinity River; thence up the Trinity River to the mouth of the south fork of said Trinity River, running along the eastern side of the said south fork, one hundred feet above high water mark to the mouth of Grouse Creek; and thence in a due south direction to the fortieth degree of north latitude; and thence due west to the Pacific Ocean, and three miles therein; and thence north to the point of beginning."

There seemed to be a squabble over the southern boundary of Humboldt, when Mendocino County broke away from Sonoma County and organized separately in 1859. Mendocino encroached on Humboldt. Instead of the boundary line between the two being placed upon the fortieth parallel of latitude as it was previously, now it was located along "the line of the fifth standard north of the Mount Diablo Meridian," which was three or four miles north of the earlier line. This modification was met by a protest from the people of Humboldt since it gave the harbor at Shelter Cove to Mendocino County.

Within a year, the state legislature placed the boundary between Humboldt and Mendocino Counties back on the fortieth parallel. If you look at the County Assessor's maps today, you will see they are still kind of screwed up with questions about jurisdictional boundaries. To Hen, lines on a map, legislators, and county tax revenues are meaningless. The only thing on her mind is that it's spawning time.

## THOMPSON CREEK

Within a quarter mile Henrietta approaches Thompson Creek and rain is falling hard. As the downpour increases, Hen looks for shelter. And so it is that she turns west and glides into the mouth of Thompson Creek.

This stream drains nearly four square miles and has excellent gravel for spawning. Henrietta's time is near and she is feeling amorous. She finds an exciting reason for venturing no further than Glynn Falls. This location received its name from Mr. Glynn, who once had a cabin here. The falls are a feature worth remarking about, but are not really a barrier to fish who want to go above them. Henrietta doesn't want to go above them.

If, by some chance, a voyeur were to look deep into the pool at the bottom of the waterfalls, it is quite possible that he would see two salmon swimming in circles. It is at this location Hen meets Buck, a romantic forty-pounder. Hen is smitten by this hook-nosed Romeo, and captivated by his tall tales. You, as a critical reader, might suggest that fish have only one tail. One tale coming up!

The story goes like this. One of Buck's famous ancestors darted up Thompson Creek in the middle of a severe storm. She overshot her destination and continued a little further than she should have. She reached Thompson Creek meadow, which now, because of the deluge, was a virtual lake. Not liking it much, she edged over into a gentle current flowing from that body of water. This was Thompson Creek, but unfortunately for her it was West Thompson and no longer part of the Mattole watershed. It was heading the wrong way. Down and down she tumbled. Soon she was in Whale Gulch, and the next thing she knew, she was in a much larger body of water. Welcome back to the Pacific Ocean! She now had to do it all over again. I know what you or I might have said at a time like this, but to put it delicately, Buck's kin merely said, "Ah, shucks," and swam north toward the mouth of the Mattole once again.

Further documentation for the plausibility of this story involves the home of Nancy Peregrine, located in the Thompson Creek meadow. Outside of her home is a small puddle named after her daughter Jessica, who used to play in it as a little girl. When it rains hard, the water in Jessica's Puddle runs both east into Thompson Creek, and west into Whale Gulch. Fortunately, Henrietta doesn't have this dilemma on her mind right now. Let's return to her quickly before we lose track of her whereabouts.

Whether from the excitement of the storm or the closeness of Buck swimming by her side, Hen suddenly realizes her time has arrived! This is it! Her main concern now is to find the best nearby spawning gravel that she can. She and her companion take advantage of the rising water and head back out into the mainstem Mattole to locate that special spot.

You might be wondering if I'm going to tell you precisely how Thompson Creek got its name. Sorry, but I'm not. Nobody likes to admit defeat, but after spending many hours brooding over volumes of tattered records in the County Recorder's office, I have to honestly say that I don't know. I did turn up some possibilities though which I don't mind relating for you to ponder over.

Sallie W. Thompson, Joseph Thompson, and Reuben L. Thompson were all granted land under the early homestead provisions. They were probably all related, and the property they owned was within a few miles of each other, and within four to ten miles from Thompson Creek.

Sallie was the first, with 160 acres patented to her by President Benjamin Harrison in 1890. She was also the closest, being due east about four miles from Thompson Creek. Next came Joseph in 1896, with 160 acres located about ten miles to the northeast. Finally, Reuben secured 80 acres within eight miles in 1908.

I feel uncomfortable with the length of distance away from Thompson Creek. I have usually insisted on residency in or very near the tributary, ridge or geographic feature in question. However, one point to keep in mind is the fact that during the late 1800's, there were very few settlers anywhere in this region. Yew decide.

## YEW CREEK

Not altogether historical, but possibly interesting, is a story concerning one particular semester during my school days, which were spent in Petrolia. We formed an archery club. Nearly all of the bows we had were made of yew wood.

Yew Creek, the main tributary of Thompson Creek, gets its name from a preponderance of yew trees growing here. If the Indians in the headwaters of the Mattole also used yew wood for their bows, I can only think well of their marksmanship, because they provided food for their families with strong bows and straight arrows. Me? I shot arrows one whole semester and never hit the target, but I am sure it wasn't due to the quality of the wood.

## HELEN BARNUM CREEK

Barnum Timber Company has vast holdings throughout the Mattole headwaters. This creek was named for Bob Barnum's mother.

In locating name origins, as my primary job has been, I have found throughout the book that the majority of landmarks evolved as a result of some pioneer having dwelt there for some time. I now come to a complete switch of how a name came to be. In the case of Helen Barnum Creek, Mrs. Barnum never actually lived in this area. It derived the name from her only because she owned the property. Originally, this stream had been named for the Colburn brothers who ranched in this area a mile or two up the creek. One fact I uncovered during my research of this vicinity is that the Warren Timber Company, from Pennsylvania, once had prodigious holdings here, that were later procured by the Barnum Timber Company.

Henrietta and Buck give only a side glance at this stream as they glide toward the mouth of Lost River Creek. Here Hen finds a suitable bed of gravel and begins building a redd (nest) for her eggs. Her male counterpart swims up and rubs against her side. Ain't love grand! Even though our departure will be a bit sad, it's not right to disturb anyone in the passion of love, so we will leave them in privacy and continue with history making on our own. It looks like it's time for us to get lost.

## LOST RIVER CREEK

Here is a major tributary that's in the hinterlands of the headwaters. If at some time during your life you have the misfortune to become lost, just maybe you would have the good fortune to do so along such a stream as Lost River Creek. If this tributary had ever been blessed with the name of some early pioneer, that is now lost in antiquity.

Why is it called Lost River Creek? I've searched in the census, and even the lost and found. My mind easily drifts to the region of terrain called the Lost Coast. Why this name? Truly, this strip of geography between Shelter Cove and the mouth of the Mattole River has never been lost. It's only because of its rugged nature, and loss of reference to domestication that the illusion of loss is so profound. Does this not hold true for Lost River Creek also? If you have a better explanation, let's go get lost and talk about it.

## GOPHERVILLE

As late as 1923, Harold Lewis remembers a saloon operated by Mr. Hamilton still flourishing at Gopherville. In its prime, Gopherville had more than one saloon, and many travelers, no doubt, took advantage of its accommodations as they journeyed to Four Corners.

In its heyday, Gopherville had salmon on the menu in the wintertime. One man I read about noticed a huge fish in the river near Gopherville. He grabbed a pitchfork from a barn, ran to the river, and came back with a salmon weighing sixty-five pounds. I regard this tale as tongue-in-cheek. I considered

*The forested headwaters of the Mattole River provide the best remaining spawning grounds for salmon.*

myself a muscular young man, but a thirty-pound shock of hay lifted by my fork to the top of the hay wagon was exertion enough. I heard one story describing the name of Gopherville. An early pioneer tried in vain to raise a garden which was constantly plowed up by gophers. Looking at his ruined garden one morning, he exclaimed, "I declare this spot Gopherville." If you have knowledge of another explanation for this name, then gopher it.

## UPPER DRY CREEK
Slightly more than fifty-nine miles from the mouth, this little creeklet feeds the Mattole from the east side. Contrary to its title, it continues to flow year round.

## DREAM STREAM
In our meanderings left to right, north to south, east to west, and creek to creek, this little brook comes closer to being a dream of a stream than any other. This creek has never been observed to run turbid water, even during the heaviest rainfall, making it one of the highest quality water sources in the Mattole. The reason for this is that most of its watershed is composed of unroaded old-growth forest.

## ARCANUM CREEK
Arcanum is one of the great secrets of nature which the alchemists sought to discover. At least this is what my dictionary tells me. Upon making a phone call to the Arcanum Pottery Works, the great secret was revealed.
*Arcanum* was the name of a boat. Two gentlemen from Los Angeles decided to buy some land along

this stream in 1976. One partner sold his catamaran (the *Arcanum*) to raise the necessary funds for the venture. It's understandable then that the partners carried this name with them and gave it to the creek on which they settled. It's just as well they sold the boat because they couldn't sail it on this small creek anyway.

## BEAR PAW CREEK
This creek is opposite from Bear Paw Flat. Not all travelers would take a respite at Gopherville to enjoy liquid refreshments and cuisine. Some chose to camp along the Mattole in a wide grassy area halfway between Gopherville and Four Corners. Once upon a time, a mighty hunter killed a giant bear in this area. He was so proud of his deed, he took one of the enormous bear paws, and nailed it to a big tree at the campground. For over half a century, local residents referred to this campsite as Bear Paw Flat.

## PHILLIP'S CREEK
One of the last creeks in the headwaters that deserves to be mentioned is Phillip's Creek. This little basin of about 320 acres drains from the ridge along the southernmost boundary of the Mattole watershed. I had heard that this creek was named Phillip's, but I had no idea why. Most people I contacted, especially the old-timers, never heard of the name either. This is probably because it is a rather recent titlement compared to other historical origins. At the last minute, some old acquaintances solved my dilemma.

    Frank Latham, a ham radio friend of mine from Whale Gulch, called up Bob McKee, a well known authority on real estate in the area, and gave me the following information. Bryce Gray owns the property, and his brother Phillip lived there a short time, from 1969 to 1976. It's that simple.

## MCNASTY CREEK AND ANCESTOR CREEK
I was told that a dweller of these premises was so belligerent to his neighbors, and even downright mean to a lost soul who might stray onto his land, that he earned the most unusual name found anywhere among these pages. People called him McNasty.

A hundred years from now, it certainly will be interesting for a reader to determine how many of these newer names are still retained. The north forks of this watershed tributary, now under a happier proprietorship, have been acquired as a sanctuary forest and renamed Ancestor Creek, in respect for all of our ancestors and all of our origins. Whether human or salmonid, we are inextricably linked.

## FOUR CORNERS
We have finally reached the crossroads, and here is where it all begins. I cannot leave Four Corners without emphasizing an important point. Visualize yourself at this intersection with heavy rain clouds overhead. You're standing where the Mattole River originates, as rain pours down. These raindrops, along with a multitude of others falling throughout the Mattole, join together, mile after mile, tributary after tributary, to form the mighty Mattole. If you have never been to Four Corners, I offer you its explanation.

There are four roads that meet at this intersection. One road goes southwest along the coast to Needle Rock in the Sinkyone Wilderness State Park. One road runs southeast along the Usal Road toward Fort Bragg. One road leads you to Shelter Cove and points north. And, one road heads east downriver along the Mattole, and back the direction we just came.

# EPILOGUE

If you're ever walking along the banks of the Mattole River anytime in the future, and by chance spy fictitious fingerlings, please realize that these small salmon probably did descend from Hen, our imaginary friend who guided us throughout these chapters. All books have a beginning and an end. Congratulations, you've reached the end!

But wait, I just can't resist telling you another little story. I was prodded by a young friend to hurry up and finish the book. I replied, "You reminded me of an incident that took place at a neighbor's home one day." While we were visiting, his granddaughter came up to him pushing a bicycle with a flat tire. She requested that Gramps fix her flat. He mopped his brow and said, "I just finished shoeing your pony, and now you want me to work the rest of the day fixing your bicycle." She put her hands on her hips, smiled and said, "Yep, it's up to us kids to keep you old folks moving so you won't get rusty." My young friend smiled and said, "That's right."

While compiling the scattered entries between these covers over the past two decades, I worked closely with a handful of friends who contributed so much time and effort, that I wish to thank them on

## EPILOGUE

this final page.

Bruce Durbin drove from San Francisco several times to shoot rolls of film.

Randy Stemler has the patience of a saint. We worked many, many long hours typing in and editing these lines on computer. He also contributed several photographs, and even left the ground one day aboard George Barry's helicopter to snap some shots of the lower river. The map of the Mattole watershed included herein is a result of his cartographic skills.

My neighbor, Laura Walker, proofread time and time again and graciously offered suggestions. The rough draft was a grammatical disaster; now the gem is polished. Henrietta's journey upstream is beautifully depicted with Laura's artwork on the front cover.

I take personal responsibility for any errors within. My only excuse for any sloppy work is to put the blame on my four siblings. When I was but a toddler, they stood me on the dining room table one day to admire their tiny brother. Before anyone could move a muscle, I jackknifed off the table and landed on top of my head on the floor. There are some still living, that I attended school with, who will contend that I suffered permanent damage from that fall. There are others who have watched me on stage singing my own songs, who profess I may have been aided in life from the early accident.

Writing this book has been exciting at times, and tedious most of the time. The really rewarding moments came when after gleaning through a few thousand notes, Lady Luck would smile on me and I would suddenly hit pay dirt and uncover an answer leading to the origin of a landmark name I had been working on. Origins of some names were nearly impossible to discover, and there were many times I was so frustrated that I nearly gave up. Most rewarding is the knowledge that decades from now readers will enjoy the fruits of this labor, as I sincerely hope you have.

This was a stupid venture for a blind man to undertake when I couldn't even read the microfiche, newspapers, or old books! Needless to say, I could never have accomplished this task without an enormous amount of help from many friends who stood by me, and even help from strangers, who believed I was doing something worthwhile. The writing of this manuscript has surely brought home one important fact to me: life would be a bummer with no good friends to lend that helpful hand when you need it. Bless all of mine.

# Index

## A
Ab Creek, 122-123
Adams Creek, 142
Adams, Helen, 59
Ancestor Creek, 168
Anderson, Andrew, 152
Anderson Creek, 152
Anderson, H., 33
Andrews, Mr., 58
Annie's Cabin, 74, 79
Apple Tree Ridge, 55
Arcanum Creek, 166

## B
Bagley, Eli, 35
Bagley, Nancy, 35
Baker Creek, 157-158
Baker, Henry Elsworth, 157
Ball Flat, 25
Ball, J., 25
Ball, Walter, 25
Barkdull, John, 35
Barnum Creek, Helen, 163
Barnum, Helen, 163
Barnwell, Gladys, 96
Baxter, Grace, 110
Bear Creek, 20-22, 135-136
Bear Paw Creek, 167
Bear Paw Flat, 167
Beartrap Creek, 118
Beartrap Ridge, 118
Benton, Joel, 33
Big Gulch, 123-124
Bigot, Prosper, 24
Blue Slide Creek, 134
Bonnie Buckeye, 63
Box Canyon Creek, 138
Bridge Creek, 141-142, 150
Brown, Green, 98

Brubaker, Lloyd, 63-64
Buck's Creek, 74-75
Buckeye Mountain, 63-93
Buckeye Ridge, 63
Bull Creek, 3, 110-111, 113
Bull Creek Mountain, 3, 107, 110, 112
Bunnel Prairie Creek, 103
Burgess, A.A., 64
Burgess Ridge, 64
Burnt Ranch, 39
Burnt Ranch Creek, 37, 39

## C
Cabrillo, Juan Rodriguez, 145
Cady, Charles, 55
Cady Ridge, 55
Camp Olney, 98
Cape Mendocino, 9-10, 35, 145
Cathey, John, 112
Cathey's Peak, 112
Cedar Flat, 132
Chambers, Lyn, 36
Chambers, Margaret, 59
Chamise/Chamisal Mountain, 143
Chemise Mountain, 143
Clark's Butte, 133
Clark, David, 133
Clark, T.K., 26, 133
Clear Creek, 56-58
Collins, George, 19
Collins Gulch, 19
Collins, Joe, 19
Collins, Point, 19
Concrete Arch, 85-87, 105
Conklin Creek, 59-60
Conklin, Moses/M.J., 39, 42, 59, 80

Conover, Dave, 120
Cook, Charles, 97
Cook Gulch, 97
Cook, Isaac, 97
Cook, Jim, 38
Cook Ridge, 97
Coon, John, 101
Coon Ridge, 99-101
Coosic Indians, 73
Cooskie Mountain, 67, 70, 73, 75, 85
Cusick, 73
Cow Pasture Opening, 60-61
Crane, Charles, 49
Crane Hill, 49, 51
Crooked Prairie, 132
Curless, Guy, 107
Curless Prairie, 107-108
Cundiff, Bernice, 63

# D

Damon, E.C., 95
Damon Ridge, 95
Dannyville, 70, 72
Davidson, George, 146
Devil's Creek, 106, 109
Devil's Hole, 106
Dirty Creek, 102
Divorce Flat, 104-105
Doody, Mike, 131
Doody, William, 131
Doodyville, 131
Dream Stream, 166
Drinking Water Creek, 72-73
Dry Creek, 124
Dudley Flat, Bill, 89
Dudley, James Newton, 54, 68
Dudley, Mary Amanda, 88
Dudley, Mary Smith, 88
Dudley, Milton Rice, 84, 88
Dudley, T.J., 75
Dudley, William Green (Bill), 88-89
Duncan, Charles, 126
Duncan Creek/Duncan Flat/

Duncan Preemption, 126
Dutchman, The, 67-68

# E

East Mill Creek, 54-56, 68
Edmondston, Donald, 35
Edmondston, George, 35
Edmondston, Gulch, 39
Elk Ridge, 132-133
Etter family, 108
Etter, Albert Felix, 137
Ettersburg, 84, 122, 127, 135, 137
Erwin, Bill, 28
Erwin Creek, 125
Erwin, Joe, 3, 124
Eubanks, Caleb "Billy", 139
Eubanks Creek, 139
Everts, John, 65
Everts Ridge, 65, 74, 79, 89-90

# F

Fall Creek, 80-82
Farnsworth, Fred, 31, 34, 136, 139
Farnsworth Ridge, 34
Fiddle Prairie, 117-118
Finley Creek, Big, 139, 143
Finley Creek, Little, 139, 143
Four Corners, 164, 168
Fourmile Creek, 126-127
Fox, John Randolph, 120-121
Fox Spring, 121-122
French Creek, 135, 136
French, Lee, 136
French, Ralph, 136
Fruet, John, 40-41
Fruet, Israel, 40-41
Fruit Ranch, 40-41

# G

Gardner Creek, 72
Gardner, Grover, 72
Gardner, Millard Fillmore, 70
Gibbes, 146

Gibson Creek, 155-156
Gibson, George C., 156
Gibson, Henry Brown, 156
Gibson Ridge, 155-157
Gilbert, Charlie, 59
Gilham Butte, 125
Gilham Creek, 125
Glass, Mr., 32
Glynn Falls, 160
Goff Gulch, Jim, 26
Goff, Jim, 26
Goff, Stephen, 26
Goose Bend, 61-62, 66
Gopherville, 164, 166-167
Grange Hall, 25, 77-80, 82
Granny Creek, 94-95, 97
Gravelly Flat, 106
Graveyard Hill, 75, 79
Gray, Bryce, 168
Gray, Phillip, 168
Greek Turn, 134-135
Green Fir Mill, 72-73
Green Ridge, 109
Gregg Peak, 112
Grindstone Creek, 129-131
Grizzly Creek, 21, 33-34
Grooms Ridge, 65
Gudom, Absalom, 122-123
Gushaw Creek, 108
Gushaw, George, 108
Gushaw, Rachel, 108

# H

Hacker, Charlie, 129-130
Hadley, A.A./Augustus, 14, 57, 99-100
Hadley Creek, 57-58, 99
Hadley Hole, 89, 93, 100
Hadley, Lee, 57
Hamilton, Mr., 164
Harris, Alfred, 95, 153-154
Harris Creek, 153-156
Harris, Jack, 100
Harris Ridge, 95, 100

Harrison, President Benjamin, 162
Harrow, Asa, 129
Harrow Creek, 129
Harvest Festival, 77-78, 81
Hazel Nut Opening, 90
Henderson, J., 33, 42, 77
Hideaway, 53-54
High Prairie Creek, 120
Hill, George, 28, 99
Hill, John, 14
Hoist Creek, 142
Holman Creek, 100-101
Holman Grade, 100-101
Homestead Opening, 61
Honeydew, 3, 56, 64, 68, 87, 95, 100, 104, 107, 110, 113-117
Honeydew Creek, 118-120, 122
Hornback, Anthony, 37
Hornback Peak, 37
Hornback Ridge, 37
Horse Mountain, 144
Horse Mountain Ridge, 144
Horse Mountain Road, 122
Humboldt Meridian, 147-148
Hungry Gulch, 142
Hunter, Judge, 104, 127, 130

# I

Indian Creek, 68-69

# J

Jeffry Gulch, 30
Jeffry, Jim, 30
Jessica's Puddle, 161
Jewett, Charles W., 136
Jewett Creek, 135-136
Jim Creek, 68
Joel Flat, 33-34
Joel Flat Creek, 34
Johnson, Darlington J., 44
Johnston, Charles, 60

## K

Kaluna Cliff, 148
Kelsey Knob, 90-91
Kelsey, Sam, 32, 87-88
Kendall Gulch, 101
Kendall, Marion A., 102
King, Clarence Rivers, 147
King Kaluna, 148
King Peak, 144, 146-149
King Phillip II, 145
King Range, 135, 142, 144, 146, 149
King, Samuel D., 147-148

## L

Lambert, Mr., 75
Landergen, Gene, 113
Langdon, Mr., 54
Latham, Frank, 167
Lewis, Harold, 154, 164
Lindley, Elwyn, 53, 69
Lindley Bridge, Elwyn, 53, 69
Lindley Bridge, George Custer, 24, 51-52, 57
Lindley family, 101, 108
Lindley, George, 51, 53
Log Cabin Hole, 74
Long Ridge, 40, 106
Lost Coast, 164
Lost River Creek, 163-164
Lyman, John, 53

## M

Mackey, Patrick, 45
Mail Ridge, 90
Mary's Flat, 88-89
Marysville Settlers, 76, 90, 105, 130
Mattole, 14
Mattole Valley Community Center, 48
Mattole Canyon Creek, 131-132
McAuliffe, John, 42-43
McGinnis Creek, 60, 64

McGinnis, John, 60
McKee, Bob, 167
McKee, Burt, 152
McKee Creek, 150-151
McKee, Don Alonzo, 151
McNasty Creek, 168
McNutt, John, 67
Mendoza, viceroy, 10
Middle Creek, 124-125
Middle Ridge, 59, 125
Mill Creek, 28, 70-71
Mill Pond, The, 87-88, 101
Miner, Cyrus, 37-38
Miner, Jacob, 38, 48
Miner ranch house, 75
Moody Ridge, 95
Moody, Thomas, 95
Moonshine Valley, 107
Moore Hill, 24-25
Moore, John, 24
Moorehead, Philo, 96
Moorehead Ridge, 96
Morrison, Bob, 39
Morrison, Silas, 39
Morrison, Squire, 104, 107-108
Mount Diablo, 146-147, 159
Mount Pierce, 147-148
Murray, J.S., 42
Mussel Ranch, 12-13
Myers, Doris, 54

## N

New Jerusalem, 69, 79-80
Nezperce, 73
Nez Perce Indians, 73
Nigger Heaven, 113
Nooning Creek, 140, 142
Nooning Grounds, 140, 142
North Slide Peak, 118, 149
Northfork, Lower, 30-31, 33-41
Northfork, Upper, 36, 106-108

## O

Oil Creek, 106-107, 109

# INDEX

## P

Painter Creek, 150-151
Painter, L., 151
Panther Creek, 151
Panther Gap, 3, 111
Paradise Ridge, 143
Paragon, The, 35-36
Parkhurst Ridge, 105, 108
Parkhurst, William, 105
Peg Leg, The, 65
Peregrine, Nancy, 161
Petrolia, 19-21, 25-29, 31, 33-34, 38-40, 42-45, 47-48, 55, 59, 64, 66-67, 77, 80, 87, 89-90, 97-98, 109, 115, 120, 122, 151, 162
Phillip's Creek, 167
Phronie's Flat, 127
Pierce, President Franklin, 148
Piner, Jeannie, 121
Pinnacle Spring, 118
Pinochle Spring, 118
Pioneer Cemetery, 59
Powder Flat, 113
Pringle Ridge, 124
Pritchard Creek, 93
Pritchett Creek, 93
Pritchett, James, 93
Prosper Ridge, 24, 63

## Q

Queen Peak, 143-144, 148

## R

Rackliff, Clark, 25
Rackliff Hole, 24
Rail Pile Ridge, 127-128
Rainbow Peak, 108
Rainbow Ranch, 108
Rainbow Ridge, 36, 62, 108-109
Rattlesnake Creek, 106-107
Reed, Tom, 89-90
Reed Flat, Tom, 89
Roberts, Donald, 57
Roberts Hole, 58
Roberts, Lloyd, 67
Robinson Creek, 142
Rock House, 91-93
Roscoe, Ernest, 94
Roscoe Ford, 93-94
Roscoe, Fred, 91
Roscoe, Martha, 2
Roscoe, Stan, 107
Roscoe, Wesley, 93
Roscoe, Will, 93
Runyon Flat, 60
Rush, Joel, 33-34

## S

Saddle Mountain, 144
Saunders Creek, 98
Scott, Tom, 26-27
Scott Creek, Tom, 28-29
Shallard, Mike, 68, 104
Shelter Cove, 122, 140, 154-155, 159
Shenanigan Ridge, 52, 66-68, 104
Sherman, W.H., 65, 77
Sherman's Prairie, 65
Shields, Freelove, 70
Shield's Ford, 69
Shields, Thomas, 70
Sholes Creek, 128
Sholes, Daisy K., 128
Sholes, Orville, 128
Sholtz, Peg Leg, 65
Shumaker, G.E., 38
Shumaker Ridge, 38
Singley Creek, 98
Singley, George, 98
Sinkyone Creek, 141
Smiley, Jack, 32
Smith, Mary, 88
Spear, Danny, 72
Spring Creek, 102
Squaw Creek, 80, 84-86, 88, 95, 103, 107, 150, 158
Stanley, Art, 156-157
Stanley Creek, 156
Stansberry Creek, 23-24, 35

Stansberry, Francis, 23
Steamboat Rock, 10-12
Sterrit, Frank, 131
Sterrit Hole, 130
Sterrit, William, 131
Stewart, Calvin (Hap), 60
Stewart Creek, 125
Stewart, E.L., 125
Stewart family, 20
Stewart Ridge, 125
Stewart, Tom, 50
Sulphur Creek, 36

## T

Table, The, 33
Table Hotel, 33
Taylor, Moses, 37-38
Taylor Peak, 35, 37-40
Taylor's Flat, 38
Telegraph Peak, 97, 140
Telegraph Ridge, 96-97, 140
Thompson Creek, 159-162
Thompson, Joseph, 161-162
Thompson, Mary Ann, 68
Thompson, Reuben L., 161-162
Thompson, Sallie W., 161-162
Thorn, 151-152, 154-155
Thorn Junction, 154-155
Thorn Station, 155
Thornton Gulch, 90
Thrapp, Levi, 115
Titus Creek, 29
Titus, Fayette, 29
Titus, George Moore Gary, 29
Titusville, 29
Trask, John B., 146
Triple Junction, 12, 150

## U

Uncle Tommy, 26, 29
Upper Dry Creek, 166
Upper Mill Creek, 152

## V

Valentine Creek, 152
Van Schoiack, 64-65
Vanarkin Creek, 151-152

## W

Walker, Jesse, 40
Walker, John, 40
Walker Mountain, 40
Washington, Henry, 147-148
Way, A.W. (Arthur), 81
Way County Park, 78, 80-81
Weeks, Maggie, 39
Weinsdorfers, 82-83
Westlund Creek, 125
Whale Gulch, 160-161, 167
Whitethorn, 152-156
Wild Turkey Creek, 70, 72
Wilder, Daniel, 120
Wilder Ridge, 119-123, 138
Wilder, Sanford, 121
Wilkenson, Granny, 94
Windy Nip, 112
Wire Fence Opening, 61
Wolf Creek, 138
Wolf, Fred, 138
Wolf Ranch, 138-139
Woods Creek, 103
Woods, John, 103
Wright, Davy, 120

## Y

Yellow Rose, 31-32, 48
Yew Creek, 162

## About the Author

George Henry Miner, known by his friends as Buck, has enjoyed most of his seventy-one years living on the Miner Ranch in the middle of the Mattole Valley quite happy that his ancestors decided to park their wagon train where they did.

He remembers growing up in a ranching family, swimming and fishing in the great outdoors, when there were salmon in the river by the thousands, and flocks of geese in the air.

He attended Petrolia Grade School, and three years of Petrolia High, and then a year at the California School for the Blind.

By the age of twenty-five he had learned to play guitar, and within a few years he was performing at most of the dancehalls and taverns in Humboldt County, as well as picking and singing on his own radio show for a local Eureka radio station. Soon thereafter, he went to Nashville and made a record.

He can still be heard on the radio today, but now as a licensed amateur ham radio operator with the call sign K6RFE. His interest in dabbling with electronics increased as he began selling and installing CB radios, and eventually led to a successful ten year stint in the radio and television repair business for him and his wife.

After their divorce in 1970 he resumed playing guitar and singing songs in earnest and formed the Humboldt Singles Club in Eureka.

Folks that visit him are in for a treat when he takes his guitar down off the wall and sings a few new

ABOUT THE AUTHOR

songs he's just written.

It's impressive to see a blind man who functions like this. He works hard raising sheep and cattle, fixing fences and water systems, and cutting his own firewood. He knows how to relax too, with camping trips to Fort Bragg to dive for abalone or go surf-fishing, or just sitting by the river writing and singing.

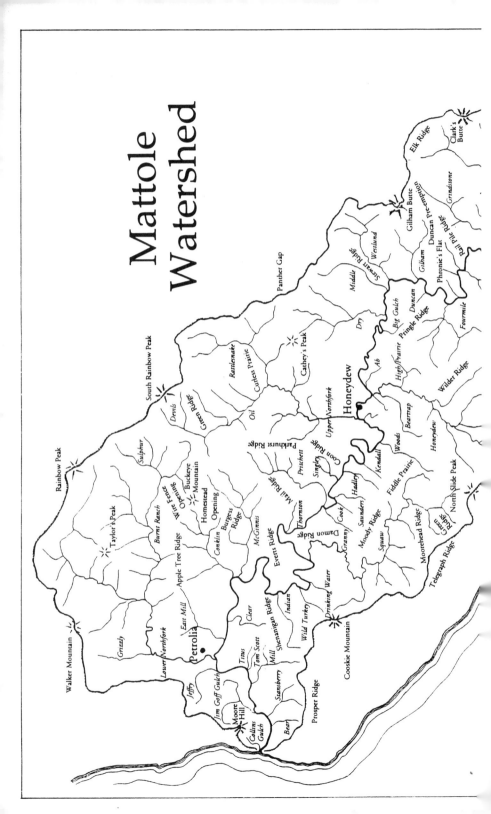

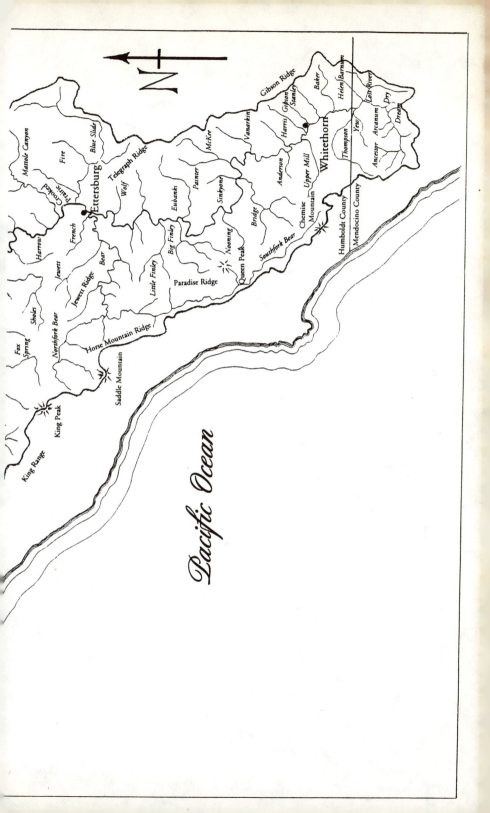